Knowledge

HOW TO BE A BACKBENCHER

Dedicated with love to
Sam, James, Alex and Natalie

Commons Knowledge

HOW TO BE A BACKBENCHER

Paul Flynn

Foreword by Tony Banks

Illustrations by Mumph

seren

Seren is the book imprint of
Poetry Wales Press Ltd
2 Wyndham Street, Bridgend, CF31 1EF

© Paul Flynn, 1997
cartoons © Mumph, 1997
Foreword © Tony Banks

A CIP record for this book is available at the British Library

ISBN 1-85411-206-6

1003064785

Cover Illustration:
Ex-Equerry to Prince Charles, Nicholas Soames
discussing Paul Flynn's Bill for a Referendum on
an Elected Head of State:
by Nuttall

*The publisher works with the financial support of the
Arts Council of Wales*

Printed in Plantin by
Creative Print and Design (Wales), Ebbw Vale

CONTENTS

The Knowledge

The village of the Palace of Westminster hoards its secrets. Education is by trip-wire. The newcomer first offends, then learns why.

The 'Knowledge' in these pages is what I needed, but could not find, when I became an MP ten years ago. Here some of the secrets are revealed. It is the experience of one average backbencher who has had a few successes and many failures. I have the effrontery to give advice on the backbencher's job as a backbencher by choice who recently had an award. As the policies of political parties merge, there is an increasing need for assertive, reforming backbenchers who are untouched by the tyranny of the tabloid press.

I offer my thanks to those who have worked with me over the past ten years and shared my Parliamentary education, David Mayer, Lynne Douglas, Tony Lynes, Robert Burley, Monisha Bhaumik and Vanessa Elliott. They will understand that in future I will have the daunting task of trying to follow my own advice.

Paul Flynn MP

Foreword

Working on the entirely sensible premise of never asking an enemy to pen the foreword to your book, Paul Flynn chose me. If Paul had been Tony Blair and I had said the request was a pleasure and a privilege you would think I was a brown noser. Well, he isn't; I am not; and the chances of Tony Blair asking me to do anything other than shut up and vote are extremely remote.

Paul Flynn is one of Westminster's sharpest of brain and tongue. His talents are now receiving the acknowledgement they have overlong deserved. Paul has a well-merited reputation for forthright and controversial views. There are few, if any, in the Parliamentary Labour Party with his political courage and readiness to say precisely what he believes. (Those who were present at the party meeting when he told the Leader where to get off still wince at the memory.)

Sitting as I do next to Paul on the backbenches I know the extent of his talents. His recent accolade of Backbencher of the Year was thoroughly deserved. I think I may claim a small part in his arrival on the sunlit uplands of wider public recognition. I even forgive him for poaching my researcher by offering her real money in place of my love and tube fares.

Paul Flynn has written this excellent survivor's guide to the Commons. It will amuse and inform; an ideal political companion for sophisticates and anoraks alike.

I can do no more for my good friend Paul Flynn than to commend his book to you.

Tony Banks (MP for West Ham) Feb. 97

The Backbencher's Ten Commandments

Value the role of backbencher as a high calling

Serve constituents, the weak and the neglected

Seek novel remedies and challenge accepted wisdom

Attack opponents only when they are wrong

Never covet a second income, honours or retirement job

Value courage and innovation above popularity

Honour your party and extend its horizons

Use humour and colour to convey serious ideas

Fortify the independence of backbenchers
against the executive

Neglect the rich, the obsessed, the tabloids
and seek the silent voices

First Steps

How to Arrive

You've done it.

Those two vibrant letters after your name proclaim that you are the Honourable Member for Votingham.

Heart a-flutter, you are on your way to Westminster. Family, friends and constituency party, purring their happiness, have waved you off on the journey that they all believe will eventually bring you in triumph to Number 10.

The first day is often a dreadful anti-climax.

There is no congratulatory call from the party leader, or any letter saying how to get started at Westminster. A veteran MP is an essential chaperone for the first day, to take the sprog member by the hand and guide the innocent around the bewildering labyrinth of the Palace of Westminster. The first task is to collect the 'sesame', a photo identity pass that will open all doors. The police demand thirty copies of the election address bearing photographs that they will then pin up behind doors so that they can instantly recognise the new intake.

A common mistake is to drop into the Commons Post Office

and ask if there are any letters. They will be hundreds of constituents eager to test the mettle of new MPs. A high proportion will be hopeless cases who have sought solutions for their intractable problems for years. Keith Bradley tells me that on his first day he had more mail dumped on him that he could carry. Without an office or secretary it was a formidable problem. There were many others. He appealed for help from the Whips to find somewhere to stay in

London. They handed him a telephone directory. The Whips believe that if the new MPs were smart enough to get elected, they are smart enough to find their way about.

A general election victor is new, along with a couple of hundred others. An MP is a celebrity in Votingham. In the Commons a mere insignificant one amongst 650. Now there will be an office, probably shared, at first. The omnipotent Whips distribute office space. The choice is a trade off between distance from the

THAT'S STRAIGHT DOWN HERE UNTIL YOU COME TO A BRIDGE AND THAT'LL TAKE YOU TO THE OTHER SIDE OF THE RIVER

chamber and the size of the office. A broom cupboard with a window above the Commons Chamber is the equivalent of an office the size of a double garage in far flung Norman Shaw, Millbank or Dean's Yard.

Those who fall for the lure of space may regret it. On countless future occasions the penalty will be a breathless dash in the rain from an outbuilding to reach the division lobby in the eight minutes allowed. Avoid the airless padded cells. Empty, they may look adequate but the free space will shrink to Lilliputian dimensions when the furniture, files and staff move in.

How to Take the Oath

The first task is to take the oath. This is not the time to display good manners. Scheme, elbow, and cheat a path to the head of the queue. The rule is 'No oath: No pay.' Until the traditional rigmarole has been said, no pay packet will arrive. Pity the by-election winners who have to wait through the long summer recess before they get on the pay-roll.

The place in the queue may determine whether the junior member will make it as Father/Mother of the House in fifty years time. Seniority is reckoned on the position in the line taking the oath. Bernard Braine owes his spell as Father of the House in 1987 to his industry in 1950. He organised his way to the pole position in the queue ahead of Ted Heath, who is of equal seniority. Braine swore the oath at 5.45 p.m.; Ted at 6.50 p.m. From 1987 to 1992 Heath smouldered as Father-in-waiting. He would have used the weapon of prime seniority to add weight to his bludgeoning of Thatcher.

For republicans the oath is no problem. There is now a precedent for attaching your own conditions to the official wording. Dennis Skinner in 1992 declared his loyalty to an 'income tax paying monarch'. Tony Benn begins his oath with the words 'As a convinced republican...'. The precedent is set for new members to innovate their own conditions.

Disappointingly, oath-taking is not a moving solemn moment. With a queue of hundreds, it is a brisk garbled mutter: 'Hold the Bible/Koran/Torah; read the words; swiftly exit left.'

Very few members have taken advantage of the television cameras that are silently recording all 650 oaths. To stir the voters of Votingham, deliver the oath in a great declamatory voice appropriate for a Nuremberg rally. Let the perfectly formed words reverberate around the Chamber in a sonorous crescendo. The rest of the queue will not understand and they will fret. But relayed on regional television, the oath will sound Prime Ministerial to the Votingham folk.

Many have regretted their frankness in revealing their full names. After taking the oath they are all published on the Order Paper. In 1992 the truth of baptismal names that MPs preferred to forget were listed, including Thain, Daubeney, Hendrie, Hannibal, Hadrian, Guinness, Gurth, Haggit, Islay, Egerton, Heeneage, Cresswell, Ducane and Flasby. One Yorkshire miners' MP's full name is Eric Evelyn Illsley.

Some things are better concealed.

How to Find a London Home

The principal need for the hermitage is proximity to the Parliamentary wordface.

Generations of novice MPs have been lured by the distant leafy suburbs. Inexorably traffic jams, high taxi fares and the

I WANTED SOMEWHERE WITHIN
WALKING DISTANCE OF THE CHAMBER
YET OUT OF EARSHOT OF BIG BEN

absence of late night transport have forced them back into central London.

Many share a flat and a mortgage in the nearby areas where most MPs live. It is useful for sharing cars and taxis. Ideal flats have a bathroom for each bedroom. MPs have a monastic unchanging ritual of leaving every morning at 8.30 a.m. and returning at 11 p.m. The demands on the bathroom usually coincide. Often a living room and kitchen are rarely used.

The village of the House of Commons provides all the day's comforts from the first beverage of the morning to the midnight night cap. For the majority of out-of-London MPs the only purpose of a flat is to provide a place to sleep. A relative of mine stayed for a weekend in the London flat I have shared with another MP for the previous seven years. When he turned on the oven smoke poured out. He was cooking the operating instructions inside. The oven had never been used.

A great scattering of MPs nest in the cheap properties south of the river principally in Kennington. The Dolphin Square flats are a pleasant fifteen minutes riverside walk from the Commons. This has long been a popular MPs' reservation for those exercising their right to rent. The maximum reimbursement in 1997 for staying in London away from home is £11,976.

How to Appoint Staff

Cautiously.

The allowance of £46,364 (1997 figure) translates roughly into two full staff, a researcher and a secretary at £10,000 to £18,000 and £12,000 to £22,000 a year. With on-costs that eats up about £38,000. The remainder will pay for equipment and office running costs.

It is usual for several hundred graduates to apply for jobs as

Commons secretaries or researchers. Generally, secretaries are long term and researchers last about two years before they venture into new pastures.

The perfect secretary has computer skills, runs a well organised filing system and is discreet, resourceful and has an elephantine memory. Patience and a genuine sympathy with constituents' problems is essential. The secretary is often their first contact. Intelligence and tact of a high order is vital.

The researcher should have similar skills with an added dash of curiosity and persistence in seeking solutions to intractable problems. The ability to scan vast acres of material and isolate the killer points is vital. The individual interests and ambitions of the researcher must closely match the political, constituency and campaigning work of the member.

At least one MP in the 1987-1992 Parliament lost his seat because of the collapse of good relations with his staff and the subsequent chaos of his constituency office. The work of many other members is marred by rapid staff turnover.

Mature advice is never to employ anyone only because they are owed a debt of gratitude for political work or loyalty. Even worse is to pick staff because they are beautiful, a relative or have aroused sympathy because of personal calamity. A contract of employment is now essential. Permanent commitments should not be made until the final day of a three months trial period.

Under the present system of allowances it is very difficult to contrive an escalating level of pay. Employees should at least be guaranteed the inflation increases that automatically are added to the full allowances of MPs.

Researchers understand there can be no career structure unless their MP is climbing up the greasy pole. Increased allowances from Short Money can be used to increase salaries for rising Opposition frontbench spokespeople. Often they are used to employ more people at dirt wages. The insecurity of the job is exacerbated by the possibility of replacement by civil servants when parties get into Government.

Volunteers are widely employed and paid expenses only. Lower standards are often demanded of unpaid staff. For a minority it leads to full time jobs. The majority have no chance of full employment. It is a hateful system. They can become embittered when no real job comes. All staff should be warned of the precarious, exploitative character of work in the Commons.

How to Vote

It looks easy but it can be a trap. Outsiders guffaw at the possibility of MPs voting the wrong way. After all the choice is simple, yes or no. Those present who abstain are not recorded.

Gwynfor Evans, once a one-person party representing Plaid Cymru, confessed that his greatest problem was discovering which way to vote. Commons language and procedure are virtually unintelligible, and there is little guidance from the Order Paper. MPs are grateful for the sheepdog herding of the Whips who direct then safely into the lobby of righteousness and truth.

When the MP arrives with seconds to spare before the dreaded 'Close the Doors' commandment by the Speaker an instant decision is necessary – without the guidance of Whips. Especially hazardous are Ten Minute Rule Bill votes, when choosing the sheep's lobby from the goats' lobby can be a gamble.

The agreed procedure when a Member votes the wrong way is to vote again in the other lobby if time allows. MPs can vote for and against. The name will appear on both published division lists. It's better than voting against the party line for no purpose. When it happens, pray that nobody notices. There is only one way that it can be made to sound sensible in Votingham: that is to say that this is the only way to register an abstention. It is.

But deliberately abstaining is sometimes the worst possible option. An MP who was passionately lobbied by both sides on the abortion issue decided to be absent on the day of the vote. He hoped to avoid the wrath of both sides. It was double trouble. He was blasted for months by the liberated women of his patch and the Little Sisters of Mercy.

The nightmare that haunts all members on voting disasters involved Billy Bunter lookalike and Twickenham MP Toby Jessel, in a vital vote on VAT that the Government were about to lose because of a revolt by some of their backbenchers. Normally divisions are over in twelve minutes. This one was being watched by millions live on the main television news, and dragged on for eighteen minutes. Toby Jessel had voted with the Government, then nipped into the 'Labour' lobby to the Gents. The Speaker ordered the doors to be closed. Trapped! Aghast, Toby ran to the glass panelled locked doors, spread-eagled himself Garfield-like and begged to be let out. The rules dictate that the lobby must be cleared. The only exit is to pass the clerks and thereby vote against the Government in the most important vote of the Parliament.

Word spread around the Chamber that Toby had retreated to the toilet and was refusing to leave. The Speaker's job then is to send in the Serjeant at Arms to prod the member out with his sword. The Government had lost by eight votes. Mercy was shown. The Serjeant at Arms put his pig sticker away and Toby was allowed to slink off.

Recently the unfortunate Anthony Coombes had the atrocious luck to miscount a vote when acting as a Government Whip. The memory of his years of toil on worthy human rights issues is obliterated. He will be remembered for innumeracy. Many votes are inaccurately recorded. Only the knife-edged ones are noticed.

He was even more unfortunate in that the clerks had perfected a method of automatically counting votes only a fortnight earlier. Previous attempts to scan the record sheets electronically had failed because counting clerks used different methods to mark votes. Coombes was ditched by an advance in technology.

How to Find a Role

There is no job description and precious little advice. MPs can go off and live permanently in the USA or the Channel Islands. Indeed, some MPs have. Their pay still arrives in the post. The amount is the same if you choose to smother yourself in over work or do nothing. The choice of roles is almost infinite. These are some of the popular ones.

Sleaze Buster
The cleansing of the Parliamentary stables is principally the job of the Standards and Privileges Committee.

Ranks will close, inertia will rule, Nolan's reforms will be diluted unless backbenchers insist on disclosure through tough interrogation. It was Quentin Davies who queried the extraordinary claimed use of the word 'want' in a vital message from a Tory Whip, David Willetts, to another. He refused to believe that the Whips communicate with one another in seventeenth century English. His questioning exposed the resistance to reform at the highest levels of Parliament.

Dale Campbell-Savours and others have long battled for transparency. There is still much work to be done by the sleaze busters witnessed by the helpful never-sleeping eyes of television.

Commons Fixture

Careful positioning is the secret to maximise doughnutting opportunities (see p.124). At Prime Minister's Question Time a glance at the Order Paper will identify those with a question. The same peripatetic MPs vary their seats in order to appear in the corner of the television screen when the lucky questioners are called.

Hone the doughnutting skills. It's helpful to say something now and again, but not essential. 'You're always there', the grateful constituents will purr as proof of your eternal vigilance on their behalf.

The Speaker rewards regular attenders. The frequency of catching the Speaker's eye is proportional to the frequency of being in 'your place'. Speaker Boothroyd once slapped down a Tory who complained because Dennis Skinner was always being called with the rebuke, 'But he's always here.'

Campaigner

The Commons is a launching pad for crusades. Every word said is magnified and broadcast, sometimes into millions of homes. A well-equipped office, intelligent staff and immediate access to the media can all be deployed to begin and sustain a crusade.

Backbenchers have a wonderful record of reforming campaigns. Politics may slide into the mush of Blagorism, where tabloid demands will discourage innovation. There will be increased opportunities for backbenchers as it is unlikely that policies confronting the ignorance and prejudice of the popular press will be taken up by Governments.

It will be backbenchers who will champion the major reforms before they are approved by the House or adopted by Governments. (See How to Run a Campaign, and How to Persuade Government.)

International Statesperson

MPs whose best friends confide to them that their talent is zero and prospects nil, still have a role.

A dozen Parliamentary organisations will value members who are ability-free zones. The Western European Union, the International Parliamentary Union, the Commonwealth Parliamentary Association are desperate for MPs with time and unused brain cells to employ. The only qualification is a willingness to devote half a lifetime to travelling, spending hours in airport lounges and hotels.

Communication is crude and imprecise. Life is shared with strangers in a fog of badly translated, confused conversations. It is the death knell for Parliamentary ambitions, but great for air miles. The penalty is to become a forgotten non-person in Parliament and in Votingham. But it is a prized eventide consolation for MPs in their final term or those that have given up or never really got started.

The main comfort is that the audience will not be listening to the statesperson in his mother tongue. Even vacuous inanities that bore the House breathless may sound statesmanlike when translated into Estonian or Mandarin.

Legislator

The most distinguished role for backbenchers is to push laws through Parliament.

The luck of high places in the raffle for Private Bills is the usual starting point. Others have created several new laws by taking over the bills of colleagues. Often the lucky winners are Parliamentary Private Secretaries, Gullivers or the idle. They are happy to unload bills on to more energetic colleagues.

Bills introduced 'behind the chair', Ten Minute Rule and

Ballot Bills can be levered into committee and even into law. Six hundred and thirty-six have made it to the statute book since 1948. But steering a private bill requires Parliamentary skills of the highest order.

Legislators are the aristocrats of backbenchers. Their role as innovators is due for a renaissance as we progress from the politics of ideology to the politics of reason.

Select Committee Loyalist

Governments need the ballast of the stodgy-brained to pack Select Committees. Objective truth is a constant threat to the comfort of Ministers. Any such outbreak from a lively Select Committee must be smothered by loyalist votes.

It is an ideal role for the mentally impotent. All information and questions necessary to feign competence at public sessions of the committee will be supplied by party, commercial or trade union interests. The flow is two-way. The loyalist may be called on to leak committee secrets back, including questions provided by advisers.

The demands are attendance and constant party loyalty on all votes. The reward is the peace of undisturbed brain receptors that need never be jerked into life. The votes of these pre-programmed minds are perpetually determined. There are also opportunities for luxury foreign travel and many television appearances as a thoughtful silent doughnut.

Happily some Select Committee loyalists go native. Objective evidence shifts their convictions and rational thought triumphs. Their hold on the job may then be in peril from anxious whips. In opposition there is greater competition for places because fewer frontbench jobs means talent is abundant and underused.

Thorn in the Party's Flesh

Those who are sickened by party timidity or political correctness can still be a valuable irritant and serve the common weal.

The easiest way to win notoriety and attention is to be independent of the party catechism of changing rules. There are endless opportunities for subversion. The media has an insatiable feeding frenzy for internal attacks. However, some MPs manage to get away with treachery. The trick is to disguise it with the claim that the member is being 'reasonable and fair minded.'

For a few with highly marginal seats this role is a calculated ploy for survival. Attracting votes across the political divide is their only hope. This will understandably infuriate the party attacked. But it will not bear a grudge for ever. All will be forgotten in twenty or thirty years.

Euro-Crusader

The Europhobes and Europhilliacs appear divided but are in reality a priesthood of zealots who communicate in a common language alien to others.

During the eternal debate on Maastricht a prize was offered to anyone who could understand three consecutive sentences in speeches by Phobes William Cash and Nigel Spearing. Europhilliacs Giles Radice and Geoffrey Hoon claimed that they occasionally understood two; three was asking too much.

Euro-fascination is all-consuming. Both sides delight in each other's company. Most MPs during the weary torment of Maastricht would have happily allowed the Phobes and Philliacs to lock themselves in a padded cell and thrash out the argument. Their final deal would have been gratefully accepted by all.

Euro-crusaders are likely to have a restricted circle of friends who Euro-torture each other without mercy.

Trough-Diver

Although Nolan is in hot pursuit of sleaze, the opportunities for cash on the side remain.

Successful trough-divers plunge their noses so deep into the trough that the only parts of them visible are the soles of their shoes. Little talent or qualification is required, only guile and a thick skin. The job is to ask the questions, fix meetings with Ministers and make speeches prepared by Avarice Unlimited plc. Recent revelations call for skilled laundering of the monthly cheque.

New evidence suggests that an exceptional mental flexibility is required. Damaging legal drugs can be pushed on the grounds of civil liberties. Murderous regimes are defended in the interest of hearing both sides of the argument. Self-deception is a potent force when lubricated with money.

There are a few new rules. Journalists should always be assumed to be carrying hidden tape recorders. Cheques for a single question should never be accepted. That's wrong. The House has said so. But it's OK to take £20,000 for asking forty questions or making a speech. That's not bribery, that's a 'consultancy'.

Constituency Evangelist

'He's a good constituency MP' is the Parliamentary equivalent of saying that someone has nice eyes but (it's understood) is not beautiful.

The hint is that an exclusive devotion to constituency matters means the Member is incapable of more taxing work. Low level constituency work can be little more than shifting paper. Complaints are passed on and replies returned without any significant intervention by the member.

Specialist pro-active constituency evangelists throw themselves into advocacy for their constituents. Complaints are pursued with phone calls, delegations and a refusal to take no, or even maybe, for an answer.

It is a worthy calling for a Member who may achieve more in his minute local pond that others do thrashing about without a rudder in the national ocean.

Extreme Wing Irritant

To the right and the left there are groupings of like minded constructively destructive troublemakers who have a pathological hatred of current party establishments. At their most lethal, they are consumed by the backbenchers' disease – jealousy of frontbenchers. Indifference to career prospects makes them lethal operators.

Advantages: fun, lots of flattering publicity, hero worship from bands of loonies across the nation.

Disadvantages: no political future/ honours/ sleaze/ promotion to the board of Freeloaders plc.

Ministerial In-flight Fueller

Known as Parliamentary Private Secretaries (PPS), they are

the bag carriers, the message bearers for the Great Ones. Their prime task is to sit behind the Minister in the House and provide in-flight fuelling. This takes the form of notes scribbled by the 'invisible' civil servants. Officially they do not exist. But in the Chamber and the Committee Rooms the Minister has a life support system of civil servants a few yards away. The PPS act as the umbilical link with them. Ministers know that when asked impossible questions in debates, stalling will allow time for the civil servants' notes to reach them.

Qualifications for the job are ambition, patience and a gift for silence. On their Minister's subject they are denied the right to speak. Hope must be freeze-framed until the call comes to higher office. Or, frequently, does not come.

Protracted silence is a cruel torment for politicians. Sometimes it is terminal and ex-PPSs and Whips have been known to lose altogether their speaking talent and confidence. Constituents are baffled and angered by what they perceive as indolence or timidity.

The aristocrats of the PPSs are those who serve party leaders. The main parties choose different types.

Tories like ancient members whose libidos and ambitions have atrophied them into natural 'spear carriers'. The man at John Major's side is the anonymous John Ward. He has happily refocussed his obsequious devotion to the Princess Royal onto the lad from Brixton.

John's duties are to be an omnipresent doughnut in the Chamber and guardian angel outside. The jobs demands Spartan loyalty and the debasement of all personal views. The rewards are lots of luxury dinners and honours in plenty.

All parties use leaders' private secretaries as lightning conductors to divert or channel backbench fury. Labour's choice is always a resourceful, talented member on the way up. Blair's PPS is ex-media man Bruce Grocott. He is a rare form of Commons life – a backbencher by choice. He chairs the group who mull over possible Oral Questions to the Prime Minister. It is his quick-witted mind that shapes the most piercing verbal missiles.

The qualification for the task is a readiness to postpone ambition, button up and harden the eardrums against a ceaseless aches from a barrage of complaints from moaning colleagues.

Speaker-in-Waiting

Unnoticed are thirty senior Members who toil on the Chairman's Panel.

They chair Standing Committee meetings and play the role of Speaker. With the aid of a Clerk, they determine the sequence of debates on bills and keep order. Mute in debate, they can vote only when the committee's vote is tied. Even then they are powerless and must vote for the Government.

The job is tedious, demanding and exhausting, with only a few rare flutters of interest. Throughout the long barren hours members of the panel stare out of the committee room windows. There is ample opportunity to watch the theatre of the flowing Thames, or to admire the architecture of St Thomas's Hospital on the opposite bank of the river.

A few may gain embryonic satisfaction in showing off their knowledge of the minutiae of *Erskine May* rules. Occasionally there are chances to slap down disagreeable members with niggling points of procedure. Most members are in their final Parliament and have given up on ambition or personal aggrandisement. A few regard the role as important and mildly enjoyable.

There is one flickering hope. Membership of the Chairmen's Panel can lead to a post as Deputy Speaker with a chance of the glittering prize of becoming Speaker. It's a very long shot, but a dream to soothe the mind during those endless empty hours.

Single Issue Eccentric

Select a neglected issue. It can be anything: sun spots, the art of diamond cutting in ancient Crete, non-ferrous metal welding, the natterjack toad, human rights in Burkina Faso.

Make well-informed, unexciting speeches with an air of authority. The trick is to be identified as that rare MP who knows everything about 'something or other'. It is a hard road. Repeated speeches bore friends and will empty the chamber. But one day it will all happen. The issue will dominate the day's news. The bore becomes the hero and a respectful House listens in awe. An indefatigable bore on Romania, found himself catapulted into fame when the revolution took place there. The hacks sought him out as the only one who knew how to spell Ceausescu.

One long-serving MP never stirred a ripple of interest in the UK but asked a monthly question about an obscure African country that he once visited. His speeches, ignored here, made regularly headline news in Africa. 'Fred Nobody challenges British Government on Obscurestan'.

Members of a visiting Parliamentary delegation were astonished to be greeted in villages across the country with banners bearing his name and crowds chanting, 'Welcome Fred Nobody.'

It pays to specialise.

Gullivers

The lure of faraway places is a constant temptation – especially for cosseted Parliamentary delegations.

Some trips are good value for taxpayers. Human rights or anti-famine forays into third world countries are gruelling. They bring the House into direct contact with the cruel realities of international tragedies. Occasional visits by those with specialist knowledge of a country or as election observers are worthwhile.

But there is little respect for the Gullivers. They are travel gluttons who are consoled by long hours in the sun at the poolside of a luxury hotel. Often the hospitality is laid on by Mega-Greed plc, an oppressive regime or environmental polluters.

Bophuthaswana was the irresistible destination for a dozen honourable Members in the eighties. They proved it by the considerable achievement of pronouncing the name of the country faultlessly. The House was perplexed with the incurable fascination with and loyalty of MPs for a far distant land. Even more baffling was the advocacy of this oppressive regime by otherwise fair-minded members.

Inaugural flights have been put on for large groups of MPs. They were persuaded that it is a sensible use of their time to invest fourteen hours flying to the other side of the world, briefly plunging into five star luxury then flying back. One flight was to Indonesia. Other very unpleasant regimes have been favoured. Try explaining that in Votingham.

Frontbench Scourge

Reputations have been built by junior Members through studied attacks on the Parliamentary stars. Aneurin Bevan made his name by skilfully savaging the reputation of Winston Churchill.

The victim should be carefully selected as a rising or risen star. Acquire an encyclopaedic knowledge of the weaknesses of the quarry. The wonderful Roth's *Parliamentary Profile* will reveal all about the vices and vanities of the prey.

Read their speeches, learn their well trodden paths of thought. They will re-visit them. Anticipate the jokes and bellow the punchline a second before they do. The successful scourge must be omnipresent at committee and chamber appearances of the victim.

Rent-a-Name

For a member with the intelligence and sensitivity of the saloon bar drunk who shouts in faces, the tabloids have a job.

To bloat out a story they often need a supporting quote from an Hon. Member. They cultivate MPs who can be guaranteed to give their imprimatur to a racist, sexist, species-ist, xenophobic, or homophobic monosyllabic sneer.

The hacks usually provide the quote. All the MP have to do is agree that 'their gibe is his gibe too'. The advantages of this role are a certain squalid notoriety with the masses.

Publicity is no longer judged to be a sure-fire vote-winner in elections that it was once thought to be. In 1987 and 1992 two of the most frequently quoted members in the tabloids, Peter Bruinvels and Anthony Beaumont Dark, lost their seats.

World Conscience

The war in Sudan in which a million lives have been lost has never captured the interest of the House. Yet, conflicts where the deaths are far less continue to absorb attention.

Parliamentary and public sympathy is kindled only when the horrors are shown on television. There is scientific evidence of the irrational distortion of the Commons' compassion in direct proportion to television coverage.

Heroic work has been done by small bands of members or individuals who have bravely visited war zones. In some cases

Commons and media indifference has been broken by their persistent crusades.

Miniaturist

A specialist group of members delight in the shrunken world of House of Commons committees on domestic matters.

The power wielded on the Catering or the Accommodation and Works committees is Lilliputian. Decisions on the shapes of desks or the number of spoons to order creates deep schisms among the miniaturists.

Their little world has all the drama, victories and treachery of big time politics in manageable doses. It is real politics. The only difference is one of scale. Many miniaturists are life's model makers or would be Jesuits whose careers took a wrong turning.

Minister-in-Waiting

Cultivate the virtues of dullness and safety. Be attuned to the nation's lowest common denominator of conscience, idealism and cowardice. At all costs avoid any appearance of humour, originality or interest in your speeches.

Never allow the voice, clothes or gesture to be obviously noticeable in the chamber. Merge invisibly into all backgrounds. At Prime Minister's Questions, never raise the voice unless all other voices are raised. Study video pictures of your appearance in the chamber. Ideally the body should have a blurred edge that links you seamlessly to backbench neighbours in a spreading blob of nothingness.

Much-larger-than-life character Nicholas Soames was denied promotion for years partly because of his love of psychedelic socks which flashed and dazzled at the extremities of his gargantuan frame.

The qualities that will secure the red boxes are loyalty, earnestness, verbal stamina, personal devotion to the party and Leader. Sexual activity should cease or be confined within marital boundaries. A safe pair of hands is always demanded. No other bits of the body should ever attract attention.

A partial lobotomy might help.

Procedure Buff

Seasoned politicians and even Speakers can be reduced to nervous fretting by the authoritative buff armed with a copy of *Erskine May*, Parliament's procedure bible. Acquiring a personal copy costs £90, though there is always one available in the Aye and No Lobbies.

A deft use of procedural traps and obstacles can delay and frustrate the cunning tricks of opponents. The House will listen admiringly. The television audience will be bored and irritated. The greater televising of Parliament has made procedural warfare unfashionable.

The viewer straining to understand Commons exchanges is baffled by these erudite wrangles. To the uninitiated, and some of the initiated, the quaint obscure jargon could be a dialect of Lithuanian.

Victories, great and small have been won by the grey people who have studied *Erskine May* and know the secret paths through the labyrinth. The 'knowledge' is relatively easy to assimilate and can by shared amongst grateful colleagues. Still, surprisingly few members and even fewer hacks now acquire fluency in the arcane vernacular.

Comedian

Richard Burton said if an actor on a London stage announced in a sing song Welsh valleys accent that 'My father and four brothers were killed down the pit', the audience would laugh.

Clement Freud and other Commons comedians have had similar problems. They are expected to be permanently funny. When Clement Freud lectured the House on the fate of the planet, grinning MPs waiting for the hilarious punchline. There was a sense of anti-climax when it did not arrive. The voice, the demeanour, were the same immutable one Clement uses for his funny stories.

The handful of original comedians in the House enjoy popularity and generous media adulation. But, many of their political talents are sinfully wasted. They are not taken seriously by their parties or colleagues. Humour rivets them to the base of the greasy pole.

Commons wit supreme Tony Banks annually receives a poor

vote from his colleagues in the shadow cabinet elections. Yet, he makes an indelible impression in all his rare forays from the front bench. When full-time Philistine Terry Dicks moaned about 'arty-farty' ballet dancer types, Tony, as stand-in spokesperson for Labour on the arts, said his speech 'proved that in some parts of the country, a pig's bladder on a stick could be elected as a Tory MP.'

Tony Banks is a deeply serious man and has made original, perceptive speeches on animal welfare, drugs reform and Chartism. Sadly, so dazzling is his comedy, his serious persona is eclipsed into the shadows.

Parliament loves entertainers but will not trust them with the serious tasks. The remedy is frequent earnest speeches on dull causes plus a curb on the wilder flights of fancy. Humour is a great leaven in the political pudding but the basic ingredient for promotion is stodge.

Divine Messenger

Effect a churchly voice and a monastic life style. Neither drink nor smoke. Be in bed by 11.30 p.m. alone with a Spartan beverage.

The pinnacle of ambition is the job of Parliamentary Oracle for the Church Commissioners, known as 'God's MP'. The models are the saintly Michael Alison or the Blessed Frank Field.

Advantages: a gain in precedence with the Speaker as the conduit for the Divine Will. The sacred messengers glow with the halo of moral superiority.

Disadvantage: avoided by sinful colleagues. The prized Parliamentary lollipops are denied, they are for those who live in this world.

Virtuoso Bore

Boredom is a mighty political weapon.

Whips cleverly incite boredom. It lowers the temperature of debate, infuriates political opponents and exhausts them. Labour's resourceful Peter Pike was once persuaded to speak for seven hours in a bill committee. With consummate skill he avoided saying anything of interest. Henry Brooke was regularly wheeled out by Harold Macmillan at tricky times in the

Chamber to send MPs scurrying off to the tea rooms.

Brilliant bores meticulously strip their speeches of adjectives, jokes and colour. They must be stuffed with statistics, complex sentences and hypnotic repetitions.

Social Security Buff

This is guaranteed. Raising a social security issue with journalists will set their eyes glazing over. They will quickly remember another appointment and scuttle off.

There are more people on Housing Benefit in Britain than have mortgages. Almost all hacks have mortgages. None are on Housing Benefit. Social Security is a fearsome, mysterious tangle beyond their comprehension. Only a tiny number of specialist hacks understand. They have difficulty in convincing their editors that the plight of millions of people on minute disposable income is of any significance.

Parliament's major recent failure has been its indifference to the record drop in the income of the poorest. The prejudices of the well-paid have ruled. The myth of the scrounger has become the accepted wisdom.

When Margaret Beckett, Clare Short and I were responsible for Labour's Frontbench on Social Security an odd phenomenon was noticed. All Labour members on the Standing Committee were Catholics, ex-Catholics or had a Catholic education.

The legacy that all can guarantee from Catholic education is an 'A Level in Guilt'. A key qualification for labouring in the social security vale of tears.

Ferret

Those who sniff their way through the tangles of complex statistics can discover the murky truths of fraud and chicanery.

The achievements of the Public Accounts Committee are usually unsung and unnoticed. Their activities are on a strata of complexity that baffles outsiders. The forensic talents of Alan Williams (Swansea West) have exposed hidden scandals in the accounts of several public bodies.

Panic seized apologists for the royal family at Alan's relentless campaign to publish the details of the Income Support for royals. Especially wounding was the revelation of the billionaire life style of hangers-on and minor royals who elect to avoid work. As a direct result of his probing, policy was changed to send the Royal Yacht steaming away from the sun spots to other destinations that try to justify its existence.

But the Public Accounts Committee can handle only a tiny number of the scandals that besmirch public life. Parliament needs a massive increase in the ferreting which is a worthy task for backbenchers.

Mantra Chanter

The first rule of modern politics is 'Say the same thing, again and again. Then say it louder.'

Training mantras for each side include 'A minimum wage will destroy jobs' and 'The NHS is unsafe in Tory hands'. Mantras are not lethal. They are the tools of the picador. They irritate and wound by constant repetition. Users must hypnotise themselves into the delusion that the words of the Mantra are always fresh and vital. The memories of the last hundred times the words have been used must be erased.

John Marshall is the unchallenged champion in deploying monotony as a political battering ram. This is probably the least demanding role, ideal for MPs with brains in perma-coma.

Select Committee Chair

Horse-trading between party Whips usually decides chairmanships. But things may be changing. Backbenchers have occasionally overturned this dangerous extension of executive power and party patronage. In a deal between the parties in 1992 Gerald Kaufman was given the chair of Heritage. As a *quid pro quo* Labour's David Marshall was to be dumped as chair of Transport in favour of Tory loyalist Alan Haselhurst. The Committee had other ideas.

Three names were nominated. Haselhurst had a loyalist vote. Peter Bottomley nominated himself and amassed one vote. The cross party majority went to railway expert and Tory dissident Robert Adley. Under his chairmanship, the Committee had its busiest and most productive period.

In both parties moves are afoot to ensure that Select

Committee membership selection is taken from the Whips and handed over to bodies controlled by backbenchers. These chairs are the most influential jobs available to backbenchers.

Whip

Whips live a half life of exclusion and silence.

It is only tolerable as a period of penance for past sins or to earn a hoist up the greasy pole. The job has been compared with the school prefects. It is closer to that of school sneaks.

Now judged to be an essential apprenticeship for future ministerial roles, many suffer for a short while and are promoted. Others languish in years of eternal hope. Some are ignominiously found wanting and are dropped from the first rung of the ladder.

The Whips are excluded from many of the activities of backbenchers. Meanwhile constituencies are irritated when their mouthpiece is muffled and becomes a shadowy figure in the Commons.

The satisfaction of the long-term whips is that of the toilers in the boiler rooms. Unseen, grubby, unloved, they keep the ships of Government and Opposition steaming steadily forward.

Mute Witness

Silence is a political device. Those rare beings, the happily silent politicians, are the infantry of the political battlefield. Where would the generals be blasting off from the front benches, without the ranks of mute admirers?

At committee sessions Government backbenchers' humble role is to stifle words and thought. Mind games will pass the time. Wallow in enticing thoughts of the rewards that will come one day...the ministerial car...the cabinet minister's leather furniture...the team of admiring civil servants...the trappings of the high office...hah...one day...one day.

Merthyr MP Ted Rowlands broke his vow when Jim Callaghan was leading the Labour Government frontbench. The scholarly Ted was holding forth at great length on an amendment of which he had great knowledge. Callaghan had previously agreed with the Opposition to finish the session at 7 p.m., so that everyone could go off to an important dinner.

Exasperated, Jim passed Ted a note 'What do you think you are doing?' Without halting his staccato flow, Ted scribbled back 'Legislating.'

Jim's wounding reply was 'Well, stop it.' Ted did. He lapsed back into the mandatory co-operative constructive silence. Ted tells the story to make the point about legislating and the frustrations of the backbenches. The prime task of Government backbenchers in committee is to remain supine and quiet. Just lie back, empty the brain, think of the purity of the party's policies and let the legislative streamroller flatten thoughts and activity.

Tyranny Smasher

Bernard Braine banged the table. It was his favourite ploy when faced with intransigence. It did the trick. He was arguing for the release from prison of Vaclav Havel, the future president of Czechoslovakia.

Proving that there is life after the frontbench Bernard threw himself into David assaults of the Communist Goliaths. Many others have courageously taken on tyrannies.

The bravest act I have ever witnessed took place in Vilnius in 1991. Russian-speaking Quentin Davies marched across a line that said 'Keep Off' in Russian and Lithuanian. Margaret Ewing and I meekly followed, watched by an incredulous crowd of Lithuanians.

A fortnight earlier the Russians had killed half a dozen demonstrators. Quentin harangued two soldiers who manned an armoured personnel carrier which was blocking the entrance to the radio station. 'Why don't you go Home?' he asked the Red Army squaddie. The soldier said he would love to go home. 'Who wants to be here in Vilnius in January?', but he said that he had to guard the station, against thieves. 'No. No. You're the thieves,' Quentin helpfully explained. The soldier waved his Kalashnikov at us and suggested that it would be a good idea for us to go home. We did. Rapidly.

The incident cheered up the troubled Lithuanians who witnessed it. Then, Vilnius. Now, the Standards and Privileges Committee. Then and now, Quentin is my nomination for Backbencher of the Year.

Heckler

Essential equipment for this job is a sonorous, bellowing voice, a lively inventive mind and intimate knowledge of the victim. The voice must amplify itself into every corner of the Chamber without electronic aid. The secret is timing. Aimless bawling when the House is noisy is heard only by the loudmouth's unfortunate neighbours. Choose the seconds of silence during Ministerial pauses to fire the verbal ammunition. One word is best. Four is an absolute maximum.

Study the speakers who invite heckling. They ask rhetorical questions, then pause. Pauses are begging to be stuffed with well-crafted expletives. Destructive or funny gibes will de-rail the victim's train of thought. Michael Fabricant once asked 'Is the Member as disturbed as I am...' pause. He was about to say 'about Euro fraud?' 'No, I'm relatively sane,' a heckler intervened.

Sometimes completely thrown, the speaker will desert the prepared text and answer the heckler. When a verbal interruption is answered by the person speaking, the interruption is recorded in *Hansard*. Usually a note is sent down from the *Hansard* writers to make sure the correct sedentary heckler is identified.

Hecklers live dangerously. The Speaker's penalty for venal offences is that the offender will not be called to speak. For mortal offences the Speaker may 'name' the transgressor. This is terrifying experience. The Speaker will bark out the names of the offender as if the words are obscenities. This extreme punishment is restricted usually to the recidivist offender who is also boorish and cruel. Latitude is shown to gentle and funny interrupters.

Committee Time-filler

Public speaking to most MPs is as natural as an eternal train of thought that is never diverted and never reaches a terminus. This task is to fill large chunks of time with clouds of words. The gifts are grey and marathon. Curb speech rhythms and cadences. Practice by singing on a single note until breathless. Desolation should register on the faces of listeners.

No case is known of brain damage as result of a boredom offensive. But in one committee an MP suffered a transient nervous breakdown under an avalanche of words. He rushed to open a third storey window after listening to hours of droning monotone on the Cardiff Bay Barrage Bill.

Mistaking his intention, someone asked in a Point of Order, 'Is it in order for an Honourable Member to throw himself from a window while another member is speaking?'

'It's in order,' the exhausted committee chairman ruled, 'for a member to leave the room in any way he thinks fit. But in these circumstances, he has my sympathies.'

The Cardiff Bill scaled Olympian heights of boredom. It rattled around Parliament for a longer period than the First World War. Exhaustion has strange effects on the brain. Deranged with fatigue and fed up with repeated appeals to save birdlife abundant elsewhere, I made an impassioned appeal to a frazzled Chamber at 2 a.m. one morning. It was for a life form not protected by the Royal Society for the Protection of Birds.

'The permanently high water of the Barrage will drown the mud sewerage sludge that is the habitat of the numerous local rat population. Not only the Turd-grebe and the Litter-shanks are threatened,' I warned, 'but what will be the fate of the rare Grangetown Barking Rat? This blameless creature has no society to protect it. If there was one, it would not be royal.' Inhibitions stripped away by exhaustion, I reached a depth of bleary rhetorical intensity that surprised me in defence of these mythical creatures.

To my continuing embarrassment one Tory MP was moved by this appeal. Even three years later, now that Oliver Heald is a Social Security Minister he always greets me with a concerned inquiry on the well being of 'those rats.'

One day I must explain.

Questions

How to Ask a Question

Parliamentary Questions only rarely seek information. Oral Questions never do. It is usually a mark of incompetence to ask an oral question except in the certain knowledge that the answer will be damaging to opponents or helpful to allies.

Written Questions can be used to unearth hidden information or to expose Government's evasiveness by a public refusal to answer a fair question. If information is being sought a letter should be written to the Minister. If the issue is of major importance to Votingham a meeting should be sought.

Prime Minister's Questions

The class act of the Parliamentary circus is Prime Minister's Question Time. The probability of an MP winning the lottery for the first question is once every six years. The first question sets the mood that runs through the full fifteen minutes. Opposition MPs try to bowl the Prime Minister a googly. The PM wants a slow ball lobbed from his own side that he can smash into the stratosphere.

'Number One' for an opposition MP is the equivalent of firing the first shot in battle. This is the chance to toss in the verbal hand grenade that will blow away the Government's defences. The cognoscenti craft their supplementaries with the devotion of poets.

Only the foolish never rehearse their questions on others. All questions can easily crash land. The Prime Minister spots a weakness and flails the questioner. Failure

HE'S RESEARCHING **HIS QUESTION** FOR P.M.Q?

at Prime Minister's Questions is profound, agonising and invokes terminal gloom.

As a fellow junior frontbencher Tony Blair advised me when I had my first question number one. He told me to spend the whole morning preparing it. 'Forget the mail. Forget telephone calls. Work on the question.'

Even then failure is possible. He ruefully recalled the time he was 'handbagged' by Margaret Thatcher. He had decided to surprise her with a question on a long forgotten Government report published exactly a year before his question was due. It was bound to be well forgotten, he thought.

He spent the morning with a copy of the report in the Commons Library fashioning a blockbuster of a question. Confidently he asked the question, certain that she could not have anticipated it.

Coolly Mrs Thatcher took a full copy of the report from her handbag and gave a magisterial reply that left Tony wide-eyed and speechless. Was it brilliant anticipation? Or did someone see Tony doing his homework in the library? Whichever, it proves that Prime Minister's Question Time is professional warfare and no place for the lazy or amateurs.

The champion questioner knows the key ingredients are preparation and delivery.

Devise half a dozen possible wordings before the day on the issues that people are talking about on the streets. Be prepared to ditch them all for the news item that breaks at 2.30 on your D day.

The question should have three parts in three sentences.

1. Seize the attention of the House.
2. Make a powerful new point.
3. Pose an unanswerable question.

Write the question out. Ruthlessly edit out any syllable that is not crucial. Try out the questions on friends. Don't accept polite praise. If their faces do not light up at the final 'punch' word in the punchline, start again. Get it right. Your party and voters depend on you. You may not get another chance for many years.

Try and work it out with a group. If the final version exhilarates them, it will impress the House. Ask them to anticipate the Prime Minister's reply. Then amend your question to crush his answer.

A model question was asked by Nick Ainger on the 6th July 1995, two days after John Redwood's bid to oust Major as leader of the Tory Party failed. It was the topical issue that was the sure-fire way to grab the attention of a noisy distracted House.

> 1. *Attention*
> Given the description by John Redwood of the Prime Minister's leadership as 'uncertainty based on indecision'
> 2. *Point*
> Is it the job of the Deputy Prime Minister now to take the decisions?
> 3. *Unanswerable Question*
> Or has the Prime Minister not decided yet?

Another questioner on the same day was less concise but followed the same formula. The slogan of the Redwood camp, painfully fresh in the mind of John Major, was 'No change: no chance.' It was also the time when footloose Tory MPs were fleeing small majorities on a 'chicken run' to safe seats.

> 1. *Attention*
> Is the Prime Minister not appalled by the ungrateful treatment being handed out to the constituents of Basildon?
> 2. *Point*
> Tory MPs are reported to be seeking new seats and abandoning their loyal Tory voters in Eltham, Loughborough and, yes, even BASILDON.
> 3. *Unanswerable Question*
> Is the Prime Minister's advice to all his Hon Friends with majorities less than 18,000 'Retreat now. Abandon your voters, because it's 'No change; no chance.'?

The Prime Minister's answer to Nick Ainger's question was a rambling prepared attack on the conduct of Tony Blair's election, with two verbatim quotes from Max Madden and John

Prescott. The logical link between question and answer was at its most tenuous. Nick Ainger won by a mile.

Alan Simpson used a neat punchword when exposing the embarrassment caused to the Government by the Defence Secretary's disastrous attempt to gain popularity by announcing that taxpayers will pay for a new Royal Yacht.

He asked: 'In respect of the Government's decision on the Royal Yacht, does the Prime Minister agree with the former Prime Minister and Father of the House, that the conduct of the Secretary of State for Defence was not honourable? Would it not be better for the Prime Minister to admit to Britain, that the country's best known sailor is right and the Prime Minister has been hoist by his own Portillo?'

Usually a Prime Minister can forge a mildly convincing link between question and answer from his vast prepared notes. Hours are devoted each week to anticipate subjects that will be raised. Voluminous damaging facts about the constituency and interests of the questioning MP are assembled for the red folder. The Prime Minister's red book is crammed with annotated information, laced with quotes, witty retorts and killer facts.

The delivery of the question depends on the strength of your natural voice, dramatic timing and, often neglected, positioning your voice immediately under a microphone. Many great questions have been ruined by Members standing equidistant from two microphones. This is a particular problem for women Members and men with weak or shrill voices. The timbre of thin voices cannot then be adequately amplified by the sound system. The questions disappears, drowned by the disproportionately loud background babble.

David Evans has developed a style of questioning that delights his friends. In his flat estuarial accent he mimics a fairground barker, with a descending list of alternatives. 'Not £5, Not £3, not 50p'. A lively, if unedifying performer, but mercifully not imitable, especially after his infamous 'charm offensive' at a school in his constituency.

Most Government backbenchers take the easy course. They contact 10 Downing Street or the Whips at noon, ask what question the Prime Minister would like to be asked that afternoon. The Prime Minister's minions are always pleased to oblige.

It's a simple matter of standing up straight and asking the question nicely. Remember to be awestruck or titillated with amusement when the Prime Minister gives the answer that the same minions have scripted for him.

But it can fall apart. Everyone is subject to a possible three second seize-up of the brain receptors. Have a parachute handy. Prop a large lettered prompt on the bench in front of you, have one held up by a friend or write notes on a gesturing hand. The luckless Sebastian Coe endured seconds of hell when he dried up at his first Prime Minister's question.

Oral Questions to Ministers

Oral Questions on other subjects are less demanding. The House is a tenth full and the mood is less frenetic. The question may be answered by a very junior sprog Minister. If Prime Minister's Question Time is the Cup Final, this is the Beazer Homes League. Still it has many fans, with an increasing number of Parliamentary groupies hooked on their television pictures via cable or satellite. The television audience for the most obscure questions on the Church Commissioners are watched by more people than would hear a MP at public meetings every evening for a lifetime.

It is possible to get away with slightly longer questions.

1. Attention (less important because the Chamber has fewer distractions).
Wasn't it unfair of Mr Alan Clark to say that the Department of Employment did nothing but concoct useless schemes to con the unemployed off the register,
2. Point.
ignoring entirely the imaginative, creative work that takes place in the department every month to fiddle the unemployment figures?
3. Unanswerable Question.
Shouldn't the Department's HQ be recognised for what it is; the country's biggest, most shameless and disreputable massage parlour?

QUESTIONS

No Employment Minister anticipated a question on massage parlours. Like the mediaeval minstrels whose poems were meant to be read aloud, oral questions maximise their effects by making the most of silence. Best achieved by a surprise final punchword, that hangs in the air at the end of the question, taunting and challenging. Let the brain instruct the voice that the punchword is glorious and poetic. Don't let it fade or die at the end. It will sound like an apology. It must be loud, confident and resonant.

Ideally it should leave the Minister's gob well smacked. The surprise may force him a rethink to the answer that has been prepared. Supreme victory is to induce two seconds of bemused silence or better still a laugh from the Treasury bench. Llinos Golding silenced Douglas Hogg and left him mouthing air and repeating, 'Madam Speaker, Madam Speaker... ' to gain thinking time when she skewered him with a one-liner, 'On what date did the public lose faith in him as a Minister?'

Two days after William Waldegrave said that it was legitimate on occasions for Ministers to lie, Social Security Minister Ann Widdecombe was trapped into two seconds of bemused lip-biting silence when an Oral Question ended, 'Can the Minister answer any question, without blaming the last or next Labour Government and confess that her employment figures are a tissue of Waldegraves?'

Tony Newton when Secretary of State for Social Security was left momentarily non-plussed the day after Peter Walker resigned as Secretary of State for Wales with a punchword, 'Is the Secretary of State not also sickened with his duties and tempted to resign, or do a runner? Or, as we say in Wales, do a Walker?'

John Marshall is the champion Oral Questioner. He has asked more questions that any one else in the past three years. More accurately, he asks the same questions more often than others. It was: 'Will the Minister tell the House how brilliant he has/ been/ is/ will be?' Sometimes he varies it to 'Will the Minister explain what wonderful things he has done/ is doing/ will do?'

Now he has a new theme: 'Does the Minister agree that the Minimum Wage and the Social Chapter will lead to unemployment/ world war/ collapse of family life/ a plague of boils/ international communism?' John is insensitive to the groans his tedious repetition draws from the Chamber.

Tony Banks is the Labour Champion for irreverence, persistence and originality. One of many examples was a plea to honour a great hero of the House.

1. *Attention*
   Isn't it a disgrace the way the House has failed to honour the great achievements of Baroness Thatcher?
2. *Point*
   We are deprived because there is no statue of her on the empty plinth in the Members' lobby along with Churchill, Attlee and Lloyd George.
3. *Question*
   The citizens of Eastern Europe have enjoyed tearing down the statues of Lenin and Marx after the fall of Communism. Let's erect a statue here to her, so that we can tear it down, now we have got rid of the old bag.

Only about fifteen Oral Questions are called in ministerial Oral Questions. The procedure confuses visitors especially because the questions printed on the Order Paper are never spoken. Their numbers only are called. When a Member has had no luck in the shuffle, ingenuity is required to be called for an opportunist question.

After the name of the MP has been called by the Speaker, the members shouts out the number of the question. The Minister replies and the Member than asks the supplementary. Then it is open to members of the opposite party in the ping pong calling of speakers from either side of the chamber. The best chance of being called is after a political opponent has asked a selected supplementary.

Only relevant questions are allowed. A link must be forged between the question on the Order Paper and the one that the opportunist backbenchers wants to raise. The Speaker will silence and humble those who fail to make the connection. They are often brutally cut off in mid-sentence or worse, left to flounder and babble trying to construct a connection on their feet.

Tony Banks got away with a cheeky one on Foreign Affairs.

He stood and was not called on fifteen questions. He was greatly agitated about the threat of Norway to re-commence whaling. Previously he caught the attention of the Norwegians by suggesting that they should eat one another as an alternative to whale meat.

He stood and was not called after mentally rehearsing tortuous links with questions on Papua, Sudan and Israel. Finally the Speaker relented and called him. How was Tony going to link his plea with a question that asked 'What action the Government intends to take to increase the imports of bananas from the Windward Isles?' We held our breath. 'Madam Speaker,' he explained, 'the people of Norway are going bananas about the whales.' Speaker Boothroyd was so amused, she let him get away with it.

There is a convincing theory that no-one listens to the first answer that Ministers give to an Oral Questions. The House in general switches off. They know it will be a bland and defensive answer. Even the questioners will not hear it because they will be preoccupied rehearsing the supplementary question they are about to ask.

Proof of this was provided by Plaid Cymru Member Ieuan Wyn Jones on 10th December 1996. He had asked how many representations the Minister had received on the threatened closure of Benefit Agency offices in Wales.

'A number,' was Social Security Minister Roger Evans' contemptuous retort. Ieuan responded 'I am grateful to the Minister for that reply.' As the answer was the Parliamentary equivalent to 'Get Stuffed', it is reasonable to conclude that Ieuan was not listening to Roger's put-down.

Daring Peter Bottomley in May 1986 proved the theory by dragging extraneous information into oral replies to Transport Questions. He had a bet with, among others John Major, that he could intersperse extraneous information into oral questions.

He had a question on the unpromising subject of 'Bus Lanes in London'. He gave three supplementary answers to experienced Commons performers including super backbencher Tony Banks. Incredibly he weaved into his replies the information that Anne Boleyn had six fingers on her left hand; that Burkina Faso means the land of wise men; that frogs eat with their eyes shut;

and that thirteen per cent of people share their bath water.

No-one noticed. Nobody asked whether he had gone off his rocker. He won his bet. Experienced MPs might offer the explanation that it is often difficult in the House to hear Oral Questions unless your ear is glued to the tiny loudspeaker at the back of the seats. The other excuse is that nothing worth hearing is every said in the first oral answers and there is no point in listening to them.

There are victories ahead for quick-witted MPs who change a hallowed tradition and listen to Ministers' oral replies. Then immediately zap back.

How to Ask a Written Question

The purpose of Written Questions is to

* Put pressure on Government to act.
* Necklace the executive with unerasable commitments.
* Reveal opponents' inactivity/ neglect/ stupidity.
* Advertise and strengthen campaigns with authoritative facts.
* Induce non-replies that expose Government evasiveness.
* Highlight Votingham.
* Seek facts and bring them into the public domain.

Written Questions are a prime weapon in the Parliamentary armoury. Skilfully drafted, they pierce the Government's defences. For a hostile questioner the Table Office, which processes Written Questions, can appear as insurmountable as the old Berlin Wall. The clerks at the Table Office are as unyielding as the shovel-faced guards who manned the barricades at Checkpoint Charlie.

An anodyne question is simple. Scribble it down on a piece of paper and hand it into the Table Office. It is not even necessary to use the printed pro-forma or to type it. The clerks will ensure that it appears next day on the Order Paper neatly printed, grammatically correct, decently spelled and 'in order'. On the nominated day three days or more later a matching anodyne futile reply will arrive from the Minister.

Avoid direct confrontation with the highly talented clerks. Their skills are underemployed. A battle of wits with an MP will brighten a humdrum day. It's an unequal contest. They are people of Olympian intelligence operating at the foothills of their careers. They have all the big guns and very few MPs outwit them. There is an appeal against their decisions to the Clerk of the House and ultimately to the Speaker. It's a fight where ultimate defeat is almost inevitable. Know when to surrender.

To continue the fight is to court ignominy. A recent challenge to Written Questions on the subject of Iraq was made by Blaenau Gwent MP Llew Smith. He raised the 'discriminatory' refusal of his questions in the Chamber. His reward was a searing and patronising rebuke from the Speaker. Irritatingly, identical questions refused in Llew Smith's name were accepted when tabled by other members, including me.

The rules are not always rational or fair. Llew Smith was then the most prolific written questioner. The primary rule of Table Office clerks is that MPs' questions must be rejected in an increasing ratio to the numbers asked.

The dozen question a year MP will be welcomed to the office as a rare visitor, possibly thanked for his custom. The thousand question a year MP will have his offerings severely scrutinised to detect minor breaches of the *Erskine May* rules. There are good reasons for this. Outside bodies and one or two hyperactive researchers have deluged the Order Paper with an incontinence of questions in flagrant abuse of the system. If all MPs asked the same number of questions as the five most prolific, the procedure would collapse.

The best course is to cultivate the clerks as allies. The MPs should adopt the posture of a supplicant. Only those with a perverse, twisted mind will ever understand the Byzantine rules for making questions 'orderly'. Give up. The clerks beam when asked to streamline crude queries into perfections of orderliness. They have the secret knowledge.

How to Answer Answers

Every answer will have been crawled over by expert civil servants at least three times. An elaborate procedure creates the first tentative answer. Then it is bounced from section to section to scrape out any speck of incriminating information, often of any information at all. The executive will triumph unless members strike back.

There is a bottomless bag of tricks available to deny information. The following are a few of the popular ones. Responses should be immediate.

Answer is evaded with reply that answers question not asked.
Table immediate pursuant rewording original question.
A single omnibus answer to several questions to mask non-replies.
Table questions singly and space dates for replies.
Answer refused because of disproportionate cost.
Ask what costs would be proportionate, question for new period.
Only part of question answered.
Table further urgent separate questions at three day intervals.
The answer is demonstrably untrue.
Raise a point of order / business question in the Chamber.
Answer crafted to infuriate with non-information.
Re-table similar but not identical question. Nail culprit Minister with Oral Question or a letter.

'Disproportionate cost' is daily used as an excuse to deny information. It is very difficult to argue. The 1997 maximum limit is £450. Harry Barnes was offered a tape as an alternative to 'disproportionate cost' answer. A library assistant abstracted the required information at a cost of his time of £15.

On the tenth anniversary of Thatcher's reign I asked her to list all the failures of her Government. The answer was disappointingly brief and cost about 30 pence. Nicholas Bennett, then Member for Pembroke, asked her later to list her successes. The reply occupied twenty-three columns of *Hansard* and cost £4,500. Not disproportionate costs?

In February 1997 in pursuit of the cost and use of the politicians' palaces of Chequers, Dorneywood, Chevening, Admiralty House and 1 Carlton Terrace, I had typical rebuffs. These houses cost millions to run and one had just had a £3 million redecoration. To judge whether they were good value I tried to discover how frequently they were used.

Malcolm Rifkind as Foreign Secretary obligingly said that he spent twenty or fewer days a year at Chevening. John Major said he used Chequers regularly and Kenneth Clarke replied that he was at Dorneywood on 'numerous occasions'. Pursuant questions seeking 'on what dates' they were in residence were brushed aside with answers referring back to the previous non-answers.

I then tried to table an Early Day Motion on the lines,

Use of Chequers, Chevening and Dorneywood
That this House...expresses anger at the Prime Minister's and Chancellor's contemptuous answers to Written Questions in which they have refused to enlarge on their statements that the building are use 'regularly' or 'on numerous occasions'.

The Clerks had difficulty with the perfectly accurate word 'contemptuous' and wished to substitute the mealy-mouthed 'unhelpful'. We finally settled on 'dismissive'. The EDM creates some embarrassment, and has to be followed with personal letters to the offenders and, with luck, an Oral Question.

Backbenchers who accept non-answers without retaliation demean their vocation.

How to Use EDMs

Though weakened by overuse, Early Day Motions are still the best gauge of Parliamentary opinion.

Derided as graffiti, they are a daily platform for MPs to sound off on any subject with greater freedom than is allowed in Parliamentary questions. Some have achieved solid results. A maximum of 250 words is permitted, but the briefest are best. Most Members will not devote three minutes of their lives ploughing through hundreds of words of tedious prose. But probably all Members would have read Bob Dunn's simple 'This House loves double deck buses.' Many signed it.

The two techniques for tabling are the 'slow drip' and the 'big bang'. When submitted with one signature the instant effect depends on the news content of the message. The 'slow drip' addition of further signatures will ensure that it is printed on the Order Paper daily for weeks, sometimes months.

A 'big bang' of a hundred plus signatures lead by the great and good on its first outing will prove widespread support. The disadvantage is that if all backers have been used up on the first printing, the EDM will soon disappear from the Order Paper.

The opinion of party Whips is demanded before potentially embarrassing EDMs are tabled. Labour insists on the right to hold up controversial ones for twenty-four hours. The pay-roll are not allowed to sign them and errant Whips who add their names to ones that infringe party orthodoxy are instructed to withdraw their names.

To stoke up interest in the subject it is useful to mention the number of an EDM while asking for a debate on the subject at Business Questions to the Leader of the House. All the words of the EDM will then be transcribed in *Hansard* and the Oral Question will be broadcast and may helpfully draw fresh attention to the issue.

Subjects range from demands to declare war to congratulations to Fred Bloggs for his work as school caretaker. They are a prop to campaigns and vital for ventilating constituency issues. Often they, and written questions, are the only immediate actions a backbencher can take to 'raise' a new subject.

Some of the motions are probably sponsored and written by outside bodies in their own interests and tabled by pliant members. A new EDM can be tabled to counteract a disagreeable one. More destructively an amendment may be tabled to the original giving contradictory facts or arguments.

Powerful amendments can wreck an original EDM. New signatories to the original result in the amendment reappearing as well. It is not unknown for promoters of EDMs to discourage new supporters to avoid wider currency to the message of the amendment.

One calling for an increased use of prescribed drugs was Exocetted by a detailed amendment saying that 'two thousand people a year are killed by medicines and 400,000 are addicted to them.' The EDM died. Supporters were discouraged from adding new names. The friends of the pharmaceutical industry did not want that sort of knowledge getting about.

Pressure groups and constituents have an exaggerated opinion of their value. Although rarely debated, EDMs are the important small arms of the political fight. They are seen at first only by a relatively tiny number of people who read the Order Paper. But they are the most influential body of readers in the country.

Tam Dalyell cleverly quoted EDMs at Business Questions to give wider currency to sections of Peter Wright's banned book *Spycatcher*. The rules for EDMs were then changed to restrict quotes to a third of the text. This is a continuing irritation.

How to Do the Business

Business Questions and Points of Order are widely abused.

In the Indian Parliament there is a daily 'Zero Hour' at noon when members can speak for a minute on any subject. By arrangement they can have three minutes and a Ministerial reply. It is a safety valve. Issues that MPs have not succeeded in airing at any other time can have their moment.

One day there will be a 'zero hour' at Westminster. Meanwhile the abuse of Points of Order and Business Questions does the same job of ventilating any matter that MPs wish to raise as an urgent priority. Business Questions follow the Leader of the House's Thursday announcement of the business of the coming week. Members can then plead that other subjects should be discussed. Any subjects.

The essential preliminary rigmarole is 'When can we debate..?'. But few subjects have any realistic chance of being discussed. Often the process deteriorates into party political point scoring. Unless there is a desperately urgent debate following, the Speaker is generous is allowing all Members who stand to ask a question. Speakers know the importance of this relief valve for Members.

Speaker Weatherill became exasperated with bogus Points of Order that were being used to wreck business. Skilled operators were hi-jacking Parliamentary time, delaying business and stealing the speaking chances of others. In defiance of all accepted procedure for debate he decided that no Points of Order could be raised until Oral Questions and statements are finished.

It stopped the gross abuse but created a new problem. There is no mechanism for raising a genuine Point of Order in the banned period. Andrew Faulds has never accepted the logic of this ban, and one incident proved how it cripples orderly procedure.

A few members used very unusual words in Oral Questions. Ostensibly it was to win a prize of £1,000 worth of games for their constituency. But it was a blatant advertisement for a word game that involved rarely used words. But as it happened between 2.30 p.m. and 3.30 p.m. it was not possible for the Speaker to be told that procedure was being abused for commercial ends.

The success and length of a bogus Point of Order depends on the mood of the Speaker, the urgency of the business of the day and the relationship between the MP and the Speaker. A genuine one should be explained to the Speaker beforehand.

The universally popular David Winnick is allowed great latitude in Points of Order. Commons days are incomplete without his ritual plea which is as predictable as the daily prayers. When he retires from the House the Order Paper should include a daily 3.30 p.m. David Winnick Memorial Point of Order.

The Speaker's permission has to be given for Private Notice Question or Standing Order 20 applications. Applications for them must be registered with convincing reasons to the Speaker before noon. They are infrequently accepted but are useful devices for raising issues that are urgent, specific and important.

Qualities of a successful bogus Point of Order include

* Flatter the Speaker, subtly.
* Appeal to her duties as Defender of Backbencher / Guardian of the reputation of House.
* Be Amusing. She will be waiting for the second joke.
* Mention *Erskine May*. A copy in your hand gives authority.
* Be brief. Prepare every word beforehand.
* Be intriguing. Full meaning not apparent until final sentence.
* Have a serious point. She will be impatient next time.

A Point of Order framed on the above lines was:

'On a Point of Order, Madam Speaker can I appeal to you to exercise your role as a doughty defender of the reputations of Honourable Members?

It is many years since anyone was called to the Bar of the House, but *Erskine May* makes clear your powers to summons here those who besmirch the good names of Members. Have you read, Madam Speaker, the attack on the Secretary of State for Wales in which he was unfairly described as "deluded" and "simple" and for his fine work in bringing six thousand Korean jobs to Wales he was accused of "pimping for Britain".

Will you now call to the bar and insist on an apology, the Conservative Prospective Candidate for the seat where those jobs will be located?'

In Committee

How to Sparkle on Euro-committees

European Committee A and B are charged with the task of scrutinising European legislation before it becomes law. Only twice has European Standing Committee B crackled into life. In the Spring of 1995 the Conservative Euro-brawl was fought out at this committee. For two and a half fierce hours it was at the centre of the political stage. The late Derek Enright, whose faithful weekly presence was hardly noticed, had a desperate summons. The whips instructed him to fly home immediately from a Dublin meeting of Irish and British MPs. His presence was vital. But the situation ended in anticlimax as the threatened rebellion by Europhobe Bernard Jenkins wilted and died.

It happened again in the winter of 1996 when more than a hundred members turned up. The chairman, Ulster Unionist MP James Molyneaux, had the task of bleakly rejecting all the nit-picking procedural pleas from the assembled ranks of Europhobes. A rebellion by one in the form of an abstention created Tory blushes, a divided party, rows in the Chamber and a full debate.

Alas! The routine weekly meetings are almost private affairs, disregarded by the press and neglected by the committee members themselves. The debates are often relaxed and erudite. They can be a wonderful arena for fledgling MPs to practice their skills.

Euro-committees are the British foothills for the Euro-waffle mountains. One recent report was flagged alphabetically in sections of about two hundred and fifty pages. The flags ran to section W. There are rewards for the persistent penetrators of these acres of Euro-babble.

Dedicated prospectors in the wastelands of Euro-trash can discover useful nuggets of political knowledge. It happened once in a session on fraud. On page 68 of Section J it said that trillions of Euros are defrauded by the wine trade. In Section B page 112 was the news that one person only is employed to control wine trade fraud in the whole of the European Union. Bringing those facts together in one question will fuse the brain of the Minister replying.

A hundred pages deeper into the report, it was discovered that Ceuta and Melillia were areas regarded as worthy of Euro aid. The Minister will know a little about France and Germany but will almost certainly be under informed about conditions in the remaining fragments of the Empire of Spain. The most industrious of Ministers will quake at the mention of unknown remote places.

Rumour convincingly claims that the hapless junior Ministers judge Euro-committee as their major torment. Backbenchers can crucify them with details gleaned from the grossly voluminous reports.

Those with a taste for inflicting pain ask brief questions whose meaning is not apparent until the final word. No Minister can hope to master the fine print. Joyfully backbenchers are allowed to put several questions. Unsatisfactory answers can be probed again and again. The knife is twisted in the wound. Government backbenchers should apply the balm of helpful dolly questions that give the Ministers healing and thinking time.

There is a case for classifying Euro-committees as a blood sport.

How to Live Through Private Bills

All MPs are expected to suffer one. Go to any lengths to avoid serving on a Private Bill. They are not Government legislation. Local councils and public bodies need Private Bills to authorise the building of bridges, rail links, barrages and other major projects. They are not to be confused with Private Member's Bills which have a similar format to bills dealing with Government legislation.

Private Bills are very different. Their role is a cross between a court of law and a public inquiry. They are Parliament's greatest thief of time and energy. Predictably tedious they sometimes can capture Members' interest and divert them from their essential duties.

Beware smiling Whips. The technique of entrapment comes when the hard faced snarl drops from their lips. They smile sweetly. A little flattery will lubricate the invitation.

A Whip who habitually greeted me me a sullen grunt at best, one day hailed me warmly with a hand on the shoulder. 'Sit down, my boy,' he said, 'I've got something to tell you. I'm going to get you a cup of tea.' Disarmed, I heard the invitation.

He explained, 'I've made you chairman of a little Bill. It's not anything that going to take a lot of time. Something to with an extension to a little railway, somewhere. It could be over in a morning.' He described the absolute power wielded by members of the committee and, even more, by the chairperson.

Drinking his tea, it seemed churlish to refuse. At the first session of the Docklands Light Railway Crossing Bill, the clerk told me that it would probably be over 'in six months'. I was trapped and coerced into doubling my already impossible workload.

Private Bills proceed with two daily sessions every Tuesday and Thursday for months. Vast swathes of diary dates must be swept clear. The situation is desperate. The Private Bill Members will be out of action for prolonged periods when their presence is in demand in the Chamber or office. The daily timetable has to be reorganised and the working day lengthened to fit in work in the evenings.

In accordance with the rules, the subject of the bill must have no connection with a Member's constituency. The constituents at Votingham will not understand why their MP is devoting a third of disposable time to a project hundreds of miles distant from their local concerns.

There are some thin consolations. Private Bills provide infinite scope for members to be bloody minded. Absolute power is in Members' hands to improve it or to reject the bill altogether. The Cross Rail Bill was tossed out by four individual Members for reasons that remain inexplicable to both major parties.

Bills consist of presentation of the case for a project argued by barristers in the pay of the promoters. Most committee time is taken up with objectors presenting their case and being cross examined.

The objectors are often unsophisticated members of the public trying to defend their home patch. The barristers will rip their arguments apart if allowed. The committee's job is to hobble stroppy barristers and boost the confidence of terrified witnesses. The greedy can be humbled; the deserving can be exalted. One happy diversion for bored members is seeing dire barristers getting mangled by unsophisticated but smart witnesses.

Barristers need the Members' votes and they dare not antagonise them. Subtle pressure will be applied when the MPs on their first committee are determined to go their own way. Barristers on their umpteenth bill will grandly explain 'The usual precedent, Sir, in these situations is...'.

It is a bullying tactic. The firm answer is that the Committee members are not slaves of precedence, but innovative trail blazers. There are no rules. The Committee is supreme and all powerful. On the one that I chaired a change of Government policy upset the basis of the bill. We seriously considered abandoning the bill and insisting that a fresh one be prepared. Another course we discussed was to call the Prime Minister as a witness because he had wrecked the original character of the bill.

To placate us Michael Portillo and Roger Freeman were summoned to explain themselves. They received a deserved roasting from backbenchers of both parties delighted to be in a position to have the last word in a joust with Ministers.

A service would be rendered by MPs who disturb the irrational rules of Private Bills. One backbencher remarked that Private Bill legislation was archaic and long overdue for reform.

His name was Benjamin Disraeli.

How to Shine at Select Committees

In a contrast to the show business of the Chamber, the Select Committees are blissful oases of intelligence and calm. And they are at last receiving the attention they deserve as the Star Chamber/ Inquisition/ Consumers' Court of the nation. In their present form Select Committees have been in business only since 1979.

Their task is to scrutinise the work of Government departments by hearing evidence and taking reports. This role is developing, and it is likely that they will soon study legislation before it is presented to the House.

Choose which Committee to serve on with care. Fight the Whips to secure a place. Membership is usually confined to a single Select Committee. Avoid those that constantly divide on party lines. They are not taken seriously. Their reports carry little weight. Choose one whose chair is not a party hack. The perfect chairpersons are fair minded, intelligent and have abandoned hope of promotion or honours.

Some knowledge or interest in the subject is useful but less valuable than forensic interrogation skills and Solomonic judgement. Refuse committees on subjects where Profits Unlimited plc or the General Union of Court Wanglers fills the wallet or constituency coffers with sponsorship or consultancy fees. However pure members' motives are, they will be accused of being the mouthpiece of vested interest paymasters.

There are some Select Committee subjects that will guarantee free travel to a luxury sun spot on the far side of the planet. If that's what your heart desires there are jobs going with Thomas Cook. The Gullivers may be heading for the Seychelles; politically they are off to oblivion.

Ensure that issues chosen for investigation are ones that the Committee can genuinely influence. The choice of advisers is pivotal to the quality of the work. They draft the model questions and write the final report. It is a mistake to leave the choice of advisers to the chair and senior opposition member. The value of the work of the Committee would be undermined if it was influenced by political/ ideological/ Masonic considerations. It is useful to know the enthusiasms and foibles of the chair and fellow members.

Each investigation follows the same course in private and public sessions. In private the subjects are chosen and the political horse trading is done. The only subjects worth considering are those of high importance where a unanimous report is attainable. Resist individual or constituency members' hobby horses.

The evidence arrives in voluminous reports, often a foot or two high. The Member or a trusted researcher must at least skim read it all. Scour the vital sections. Star the killer points.

Ensure that no key witnesses are ignored by advisers. Challenge invitation to repetitive witnesses included to reflect partial interests.

FIRST WITNESS PLEASE

The public cross-examination of witnesses is now frequently broadcast. The aim is to draw out helpful evidence, expose the deceivers and crush the crooks. Time is very limited. Carefully plan questions from a detailed study of evidence. Quote vital phrases or induce witnesses to repeat their key sentences. A handful of people read the original reports. Millions may hear the verbal evidence.

Some witnesses are unsophisticated. They deserve gentle handling. Put them at ease. Be courteous. Ask deliberately easy questions. Thank them generously. Compliment them on their answers if nervousness persists.

Civil servants are trained with a video called *How to give evidence to a Select Committee*. It advises them to make their answers as long as possible to ensure that MPs cannot ask too many questions. Politicians and other well organised witnesses are now professionally coached before they appear. They have undergone dummy sessions with their skilled advisers who have tried to anticipate the questions.

There is strong evidence that many witnesses have prior knowledge of the questions prepared for committee members by advisers. The Committee Clerk will have legitimately told them of the general headings of the subjects to be raised. There are grave suspicions that detailed questions may be leaked by political, business or trade union chums on Committees. This is the best reason not to use the prepared questions, especially for formidable witnesses who may have been tutored in answering them.

Show them no mercy. They are out to conceal the truth. Try to knock them off their perch with your first question. It should expose a contradiction or falsehood in their evidence. Point out, at first courteously, that they are not answering the questions. One Minister in answer to a simple question of mine spoke for eleven minutes making all the points he had previously planned to make and not attempting to answer my question. It is not the function of a Select Committee to provide another platform for Ministers.

If witnesses persist in stonewalling, apologise for being direct and discourteous, then ask a question that is sharply direct and discourteous. Often the only remedy to block streams of vacuous verbiage is to interrupt the witness. Tell them that they are not answering the question. If they still evade, repeat the question again word for word.

Richard Branson thought the Transport Committee had been hard on him because he wore a jogging outfit to address the committee. Wrong. Their irritation was aroused by his ignorance of railways. When asked in a programme connected with the inquiry what he was going to do to improve the running of his privatised service, Branson said he would urge his drivers to drive faster. 'To overtake the train in front, presumably,' was the mocking whispered response by a Committee member.

To gain media attention and a place on the evening regional news, those who ask the first questions have an advantage. In every other respect it is best to be the final questioner. The obvious and the prepared questions will then have been asked. Listen carefully to the answers, spot the weaknesses and leap on them. Note the strong points made in answers to other members. Use the limited time and insist on a second go to rebut or re-inforce contradictions.

The main faults of members are making speeches or asking vague questions. The most eloquent exchanges are the sharp single sentences that strike at the heart of the issue. Broadcasters are seeking tiny fifty second sound and vision bites to illustrate three hours of evidence.

Be hyperactive in the tedious lengthy private sessions when the report's headings are considered. Prepare detailed amendments to highlight key information. Committed members should draft their own recommendations and not rely on amending those written by advisers.

To fill the gaps in the evidence, ask written Parliamentary questions on points not fully developed by witnesses. Although reports are usually confined to evidence received, Parliamentary answers can be included.

If the final report is not good, a member can re-write it. The Committee Clerk will help. Seek outside help if necessary. Be prepared for the horse-trading. Reports that carry the greatest authority are unanimous ones. Be prepared to sacrifice and compromise even lovingly-drafted prose. As elsewhere in Parliament, the spoils are won by the industrious.

Leaking the report to many hacks who request advance details is always damaging. It will ruin the standing of the leaker with fellow members and blunt the impact of the conclusions. The parts of the media who are not recipients of the leak will strike back with thin or no coverage. Be present at the Press Conference. Have sound bites ready for both specialist and general reporters plus a fifteen second one for the main television news. The speciality subject reporters will read the details. The rest of the hack pack are searching for a simple sentence headline. Give it to them, brief, punchy news-stuffed.

Exploit the value of the report afterwards by raising the issues in questions and debates. If the issue is dying try an Adjournment Debate/ Ten Minute Rule Bill six months later. If the report has wounded some dragons, be ready with the killer punch. The prize virtues of all politicians are patience and persistence. If the vested interests get away with it, it's the fault of the inactive Committee members.

How to Endure Standing Committees

The chore of Standing Committees is a hideous shock to novice Members. Their current operation demeans Parliament and creates bad law.

The purpose of a Standing Committee is to undertake the line-by-line scrutiny of a Bill. They are made up of fifteen to forty-five appointed members reflecting the party balance in the House. A neutral chairman takes the place of the Speaker of the House. Members stand to move and debate new clauses and amendments. They can take anything from one sitting to several months to get through a Bill depending on its length and controversiality.

A new Member is press-ganged on to one usually in the first month of arriving in Parliament. Immediately the already full day's workload is doubled with committees that demand huge chunks of time. Morning sessions run from 10.30 a.m. to 1 p.m., afternoons from 4.30 to 7.30 p.m., sometimes evening sessions from 9 p.m. to any time.

Government backbenchers are the winners. All that is required of them by the Whips is their constant attendance and dutiful voting. Speaking is a time wasting obstacle to the speedy passage of Government Bills, the only task of Standing Committees. Government MPs learn how to productively fill their time by opening the mail and writing replies.

Opposition MPs are lectured that their only influence is the ability to delay Government bills. They are urged to fill time spaces with words whose main purpose is obstruction. Improvements are attempted to bills, but rarely are they accepted by the elective dictatorship of Government. Standing Committees are political battlegrounds not rational instruments of reform.

This system produced the Child Support Agency and the law that allowed SERPS good value state pension scheme to be wrecked in favour of personal pensions that have robbed millions. Minutes of the debates are shaming to most Committee members on those Standing Committees. Few foresaw the consequences of their decisions.

A real challenge to backbenchers is the reform of Standing Committees from the arrogance of ideological bullying to intelligent enlightened debate. Andrew Marr in his splendid book *Ruling Britannia* describes the futility and damage of Standing Committee procedures and suggests needed reforms. They should be promoted. Only backbenchers will do that.

The Office

How to Knock-out the Mail

Throughout the year the brown tide of letters pours in. The basic weapons for mail warfare are a paper knife and a large waste paper basket – known in the trade as 'the circular file'. Be prepared to be ruthless.

One MP has an enviable if dangerous formula. All letters in large brown envelopes, or that have post marks other than Votingham are dispatched unopened to the circular file. He has a majority of 18,000.

Others sort the letters. The obvious junk advertises itself with a logo on the envelope or now helpfully in a transparent package. Totally urban Votingham absolves its Member from the task of opening the week's dozen press releases from the National Farmers' Union or the personal free copy of the *Slurry Gazette*.

ONE FOR YOU, ONE FOR ME....

My rough guide to staff is that letters worth a glance are from the numberless causes – bad and good.

Bad are lobbyists, tobacco companies, drug firms, annual reports from privatised firms, the road lobby, and campaigns to restore King Rupert to the Throne of Bulgaria.

Good are charities, environmental groups, voluntary bodies, and campaigns to reform monarchies and end drug prohibition.

The prized letters are hand written with a Votingham postmark. These are from real human beings often with serious problems. Generous time is devoted to them.

How to Write a Standard Letter

Standard letters are always second best. They are often the written equivalent of a two fingered sign. Send them rarely to constituents except in return to a standard letter writing campaign directed at the MP. Even then, a few personal words should be added. However when the office is overstretched they are the only way to send out information rapidly and efficiently.

If the letter to the MP was written by a computer, the MP's computer should reply. Standard printed cards and messages are available. Their use was justified in the bad old days of mechanical typewriters and few staff. Less so now.

How to Write an Abusive Standard Letter

For those who request you to do something that is light years distant from your political stance a direct simple message will suffice:

> Thank you for your communication which I placed in my insane letters file.

Lobbyists are more difficult to shake off because they are professional naggers. Generally they are not deeply subtle and understand only a blunt reply. A formula I have found useful is:

> Dear Lobbyist,
> I know of no good reason why I should co-operate with your inquiry. Lobbying organisations such as yours are an ugly, anti-democratic and corrupting incubus that haunts the British body politic.
> If your client is genuinely seeking information I would be happy to provide it after they have directly approached me. Using you as a conduit only adds to their costs for no worthwhile purpose.
> The quicker your malign presence is expelled from Westminster the sooner the cleansing of the Parliamentary stables will begin.

Drug companies are difficult to repel partly because they are convinced that all MPs are scientific morons. When Drug Pushers plc urge backing for their campaign to deluge the country with more expensive, unnecessary toxic medicines, they should be vigorously challenged

In reply to one reasonable request I made for scientifically respectable arguments to back a claim they sent me copies of personal testimonies from individuals that had all the intellectual authority of a baked bean advert. Their transcendent greed jumped from every word of their odious letters.

Of course, it is not always necessary to be as mealy-mouthed as I am.

How to Deal With Insane Letters

Those who are slightly mad, eccentric or possessed by demons are magnetically attracted to MPs. The obsessive, the weirdos and devotees of religious cults ventilate their irrationality at great length and frequency to Members.

Never give them a morsel of encouragement. Politely and non-provocatively deflect the majority off to their own constituency MPs. Patently unreasonable requests sent to all MPs can be justifiably and wisely thrown out, without acknowledgement.

Among ones received in a typical six month's mail are,

Victim of Mafia oppression in South Hendon.

The world's ONLY perpetual motion invention.

Tony Blair is a reincarnation of Adolf Hitler.

Request for a financial donation for a gift to the Queen – *World Without Hunger Organisation.*

Racialism is patriotism – *Leaflet.*

All documents at the National Library of Wales are forged – *letter.*

I am being poisoned/ persecuted/ spied on by the Catholic Church/ MI5/ Baptists/ New Labour – *various letters.*

Almighty God has instructed me to write to all MPs – *letter.*

Princess Diana is possessed by Satan – *letter.*

Tobacco advertising cuts tobacco use – *The Advertising Association.*

My uncle, a famous actor, made me pregnant when I was two years old – *letter*.
Soul Eater Incidents Increase – *The Think for Yourself Movement*.
The wrath of God will be visited on Welsh Water – *letter*.
Our data-base will allow us to return to the time of Christ – *circular*.

The Votingham ones must be handled with care. They will know the home telephone number, possibly even the home address. One MP has become resigned to having a visit from his tame eccentric at every surgery. For him a firm line is now too late. Most Members regret that early tolerance of the eccentric and the slightly deranged encourages a career-long persecution that becomes inescapable.

Others are possibly mentally ill. Unless they are constituents who can be ushered into situations where they can be advised or cared for, it is generally counter-productive to enter into any detailed correspondence.

How to Cull Invitations

Devise a scientific equation for evaluating invitations. Try asking these questions of all invites.

A = Why me?
B = What's to be gained for me/ constituents/ party/
    campaigns?
C = What is the cost in time and disruption to my
    working day?
D = Damage to waistline/ liver/ reputation

The equation is
$(A + B) + (C + D) = X$

When X is positive, Accept.
When X is negative, Refuse.

If that is too complex the following instant reckoner may help.

Receptions

Commercial bodies out to bend the ear through offers of food and drinks. They can be mildly enjoyable social events but are guilt-inducing wastes of time. Say 'no' and ask for a written report on the points they want to make. *Hot tip.* If 'Champagne' is mentioned in the invitation, say no. Their business is bribery.

Charities. Sometimes worthwhile if there are contacts that need strengthening but almost always a phone call or a letter is a more efficient way of gaining knowledge. *Hot Tip.* If financial contribution is asked to pay for the hire of the room, they are likely to be a serious cost-conscious body. Accept.

Campaigns. Can be useful if they show a film or convey an inspirational message. *Hot Tip.* Some tired campaigns are vastly oversubscribed by dozens of MPs. Best to try the novel cause with a fresh message that challenges accepted wisdom.

Conferences

Most are all day affairs outside of Parliament. Booking in advance may result in a painful absence from a major but unplanned Parliamentary event. Rarely is the windy rhetoric of a conference worth a whole day. Experience teaches that only about a fifth of conference speeches contain new material. Sometimes less. The valuable knowledge can be gleaned in ten minutes from a written report. Often ludicrously expensive fees are demanded.

Lunches

Journalists. Frequently worthwhile if the journalist's work is known to you. Can be useful in gaining knowledge, and socially refreshing. Never relax if the journalist is a stranger or from a politically hostile paper. They are working, not relaxing. A manoeuvre is to feign indiscretion and confidentiality in order to coax similar response from the MP. It's a trap set to damn. *Hot tip.* Insist on picking up the bill for the first meal and every alternative one. Never lunch with more than one journalist – they will gang up on the MP in their account of what was said. They will convincingly outnumber the member – as Steve Byers discovered when hacks followed a meal with him by each publishing a piece on Labour's 'embarrassing Union plans. They caucus together and agree the common line that becomes the proclaimed truth. As Byers discovered it is very difficult to be convincing in disagreement with unanimity from the hack pack.

Overseas Visitors. A very valuable use of time is to meet visiting Parliamentarians from countries of specialist interest. Hassle-free arrangements are made by the Foreign Office. All the time is spent in contact with usually very senior politicians. This is the most amenable and time efficient way to explore foreign issues. *Hot tip*. Some knowledge of English is universal but variable; use interpreters freely when misunderstandings are suspected.

Constituents and Campaigners. The best way of saying thanks, but can rarely be used because of the pressures on time.

Meetings

All Party Parliamentary Groups. The hundreds of all party groups need at least five Government and five Opposition members. Almost every country in the world has its gang of devotees. Some are serious. Many exist to facilitate dinners at the Embassy or to give a leg-up for a place on delegations visiting foreign countries. Groups on issues such as disability or alcohol abuse are dynamic, successful lobbyists for good causes. Others are commercially based and shamelessly promote self-interest. Reputations have been built by otherwise useless members pontificating in the media as an officer of 'All Party Cetacean/ Vegetarian/ Esperanto Appreciation Group'. In common with most groups, it probably meets once only a year for an Annual General Meeting with officers only present.

Explore the 'support' given to groups that lobby for commercial interests. Although the rules have been changed, many continue as extensions of lobbying and are pursuing their paymasters' murky aims.

Party Backbenchers Groups. They often have a shadowy, transitory existence. They are used as a tentacle of control to be jerked when required by Opposition Whips. Government find them useful as lightning rods for grounding dissent. *Hot tip*.

Generally underused by backbenchers as instruments for improving policy.

How to Delegate

It is impossible to accept all invitations even from worthy causes.

MPs' staff must be allowed moments in the flattering limelight of publicity. Selfishness is a deplorable trait in bosses. Staff appreciate chances to take the place of Members who are asked to parachute, bungy jump or abseil down buildings in the support of a good cause. Staff are generally younger and cope with physical challenges while Members concentrate on growing old decorously. One MP did not delegate a parachute jump. He lived to tell the painful tale, but still has a persistent nasty injury.

Researchers should be liberated to pursue their own enthusiasm and attend briefings in place of their bosses. Well-informed, and passionately motivated staff will deliver work of high quality. In some offices press feature articles are written by staff with specialist knowledge and published under the name of the member. Very often it ends in tears. The Member's superficial knowledge is painfully exposed by diligent press questioning.

It can work the other way around when an MP has specialist knowledge in a subject. Outsiders assume cretin abilities for all MPs and quiz researchers as the founts of all wisdom. Gifted staff write speeches which are sometimes delivered verbatim by Members. It's a dangerous game. Interventions will crack the egg shells on which the Member is treading. It is painful to witness Members floundering, exposed because they do not understand the speech they are making.

A thorough knowledge of themes is achieved by slaving over a wordprocessor writing speeches and articles from notes gathered by staff.

Cabals of researchers gather to exchange horror stories about their bosses. The stereotype is of a lazy, vain overpaid prima donna who feeds off the labours of starving minions. The highest tribute an employer MP can earn is the enduring respect of employees.

How to be Reported

The *Hansard* writers buttress their great skills with uncanny intuition. Never once has a Member made a grammatical mistake. Even hopeless gibberish appears as cogent argument. Missed words and even lines in quotations miraculously reappear. All MPs owe the *Hansard* staff a debt of gratitude.

But they are not perfect. Once I said that Welsh Ministers and the Welsh Office were moving in contrasting directions. *Hansard* recorded my saying 'The Welsh Office is building concrete erections'.

A reference to the village of Undy in Gwent prompted a note from on high 'The village of Undie ? ? ?' Nick Ainger praised the Welsh language film *Hedd Wyn*. 'Head wind' was printed. William Mckelvey once sang a question which went 'You've never smelt the Tangle of the Isles'. To Tam Dalyell's discomfort, it was reported as 'You'll never smell the Tam of the ailes.'

There have been triumphs. Finishing a speech one day I quoted some obscure lines from Chaucer, 'If gold rusts, what will iron do?'. A hour later I called in to check the speech and the verse was printed with correct Chaucerian spelling.

Speeches of any substance are always worth checking. Even the most skilled speakers sometimes say the wrong words, omit a vital 'not' or mumble indistinctly. Corrections to the *Hansard* text must be swift or the mistake will grow legs.

Copies of speeches are very useful to explain a Member's stance on issues especially when they are correct in every detail. They are extremely useful in sending to inquirers and constituents and avoid a great deal of unnecessary letter writing.

How to Use the Library

The Commons Library is a life support system, an archive, an inspiration and a place to rest and snooze.

No reasonable request is ever denied. Given time, the band of experts produce detailed briefs, informative press cuttings and past *Hansard* quotations. When the media are screaming out for urgent interviews, updates on half-forgotten issues can be produced in a few hours.

It's risky to delay queries. Never is it fair to ask for a briefing on a question or a debate with less than three days notice. There is usually only one member of staff for each specialist subject and ample time must be allowed. The quality of the work produced will depend on the Member's relationship with the librarians. Never commit any of their seven sins.

Seven Library Sins

* Asking for information and not collecting it from the tray.
* Demanding more information than necessary.
* Repeating requests for identical material within a brief period.
* Not turning up for debates/ questions on which you have briefed.
* Asking staff to research subjects outside their expertise.
* Expecting librarians to do the work of MP's researcher/ political party/ secretary.
* Never saying thank you.

Increasingly Members' offices are being plugged into the improving Parliamentary databases. Make the most of them. The power to delve and select from an MP's desk nuggets from the vast information treasure chests adds to efficiency. But the system is slow, inefficient and exasperating. Only pressure from MPs will improve it.

Library Fact Sheets and P.O.S.T. reports can be read and printed from a screen in the Members' offices. The vast information prairies of the Internet can be explored using the same link. Only occasionally is it as efficient and as useful as traditional means in gathering information and news.

The wonder of electronic mail was once used to interrupt my work on a monitor with messages saying 'Jane, we're eating at Fat Cops, today. See you there, Alex.' The message came from a work station in a neighbouring office, two minutes walk away. E-mail is becoming the new medium for exchanging office gossip eliminating the chore of standing up and walking a few yards.

The really useful technological leap is that *Hansard* is now available on CD ROM. To receive the discs Members have to abandon their rights to receive the weighty, handsome bound tomes. They are difficult to use but look great in large numbers as a backdrop for television interviews.

The main Library is agreeably little changed from its traditional role. The presence of newspapers, Ceefax and computers do not detract from its hushed atmosphere, reminiscent of libraries in the great universities. For about fifty regular attenders, the Library is refuge of peace. Before the days of individual offices, Members worked from desks there. Dozens still find it the most congenial, phone-free haven for serious work and study.

The most comfortable armchairs in the Palace are in a semi circle around the now decommissioned fireplaces. Regulars gather there in growing numbers throughout the tiring Parliamentary day to read and snooze. Only the division bells are allowed to disturb the peace.

How to Allocate Time

Parliamentary time is not equally rewarding in achievement, publicity or benefit to humankind. Long hours of exacting toil on Bill Committees will be rewarded in heaven only. Three sentences of inspiration at Prime Minister's Question Time elevates the unknown members to heroic status among their peers and quickens the pulses among the constituents.

The Votingham Standard Guide to the value of MP time is:

30 seconds of PM Question Time =
20 minutes of Oral Questions =
3 hours of Select Committee questioning =
28 hours of continuous backbench speeches in the Chamber =
2 months of speaking in Standing Committees =
28 years speaking on European Standing Committee B =
78 years on Committees on Statutory Instruments

How to Run a Campaign

Out of the dreary mulch of humdrum work a Surtsey of an

70

issue will occasionally arise, sparkling and explosive. It may be a mountainous injustice, a mire of corruption, or a wasteland of stupidity.

A campaign issue must be:

* Capable of practical solution by Parliamentary action or pressure.
* Likely to engage significant public sympathy.
* A slayer of dragons or an uplifter of the dispossessed.
* A boost to the sum of human happiness/ safety/ ecstasy.

The stages are:

Research. Use the Commons Library and pressure groups to explore the issue. Seek information from allies and foes to test strengths and weaknesses. Write down the case, fashion the sound bites. Interest feature writing journalists in the fine details.

Launch. A Prime Minister's Question is a dream chance to launch the campaign. Next best are a Ten Minute Rule Bill or an Adjournment Debate, especially one on Wednesday morning when more time is available. Send out an embargoed press release with irresistible tasters that intrigue and excite jaded hacks to seek more.

Arrange a press conference in the Jubilee Room (one of few rooms where television cameras are allowed) with witnesses in attendance. Celebrities are useful, but better are those offering powerful personal testimony to back the message. A trim message is needed to fit the available time slot. In an adjournment debate enlist speeches from other MPs. Political opponents are useful. Even a minute's contribution from three of four MPs with high reputations greatly strengthens the case.

Media. Clear the decks of all other commitments to cope with press interest. If overwhelmed, ensure that your secretary has a clear idea of news values. It's a sickening experience to be informed 'Because you're booked for interviews on Radio Hull and Radio Ceredigion, I told *Newsnight* that you could not come to their studio'. If the media want a superstar MP to present the case, don't stand in the way. The issue is supreme, not your vanity.

Long Haul. After the big bang of the presentation there will be a fading afterglow of interest for a few days. Then the real campaigning starts. Unleash a measured but persistent onslaught of Parliamentary speeches, questions, EDMs. Organise a press campaign of news plus letters seeking information and cases to support the cause. The neglected five hundred regional newspapers will often co-operate. Some may adopt your campaign as their own.

Write to Ministers and the Prime Minister with requests for detailed information. Make the subject a nuisance that the Minister longs to expel from his daily red box. Buttonhole him occasionally in the lobbies. Judge success by the hunted look in the ministerial gaze. When they become offensive, or better still insulting, success is near.

Woo support from other MPs, outside organisations, the Library and the political party. Persuade them to supply you with news of helpful developments. Bombard the Chamber with Business Questions, Points of Order or opportunistic Oral Questions contrived to back your campaign.

Hail any partial victories. Chart your weekly 're-launches' of the campaign to coincide with media fallow times – Mondays, Fridays, recesses and Bank Holidays. Never falter. Frequent knocking splits the stone.

If publicity is carefully targeted and repeated, policy can be changed even if new legislation has not gone through the House. Grow a thick skin, fellow MPs groan in weariness of the repetitions on the theme, but respect persistence and know its value.

Keith Lockwood, Manager: Government affairs at Vauxhall, said in February 1997

> Discounting the role and impact of House of Commons backbenchers is naive and shortsighted. We only have to study the impact one backbencher had on the behaviour of the British motor industry on a 'safety issue.' It would be true to say that whilst Vauxhall acted quicker than most, the whole automobile sector has now moved to tackle the problem without a single new law being passed. Media opinion has also turned against the use of these products. Advertising too! The backbencher took a lead.

Industry followed. Powerful stuff for a mere backbencher.

The safety measure itself was 'talked out' by a Government Minister following by a debate that had all-party support. Legislative failure was translated into a safety success through the Parliamentary megaphone of publicity.

How to Deal with Disaster

Local disasters propel obscure backbenchers into immediate fame. Instant authority and pre-eminence in debate is bestowed by a generous House on the local Member. Reputations are made or destroyed.

Nick Ainger, the resourceful Member for Pembroke, was placed at the centre of one of the worst ever pollution incidents. The beaches and wildlife of his beloved constituency were blanketed in oil from the grounding of the *Sea Empress* tanker.

In a bravura performance Nick was regularly speaking live from St. Anne's Head on breakfast news and arguing the case 240 miles away in Parliament six hours later. As a model constituency MP he had an encyclopaedic knowledge of his constituency's industries. He had lived in Pembroke for many years and knew the Milford docks at first hand. The delicate balancing act he had to perform was to highlight the massive pollution, to secure new safety measures without frightening off the summer visitors on which the prosperity of his constituency depends.

Another relatively unknown MP was forced into prominence by tragedy. The heartbreaking and avoidable deaths of schoolchildren in a canoe accident involved constituents of David Jamieson of Plymouth Devonport. His previous career in education equipped him to engage the sympathy of the House. Building on the errors of the tragedy he has led an educational initiative to properly train those who work in children's leisure activities. These are solid achievements of reform created from adversity by a backbencher

The least likely Commons star was the genuinely modest Mark Wolfson. He is one of the most unlikely characters in politics because of his unassuming personality. He has no enemies and was thought to be destined for inescapable anonymity. Britain's worst storm in 1990 reduced his Sevenoaks constituency to One Oak. It was Mark who emerged from the shadows and acquitted himself superbly well.

These three are splendid models for all backbenchers faced with disaster. Others have failed. Some overplayed minor incidents or downplayed serious ones. Others were caught short on unjustifiable trips abroad when disaster struck.

How to Eat and Drink

Simply. There is a persuasive army of people bent on bloating the bodies and dulling the senses of Members with fine food and drink. They aim to induce states of comatose receptivity to their blandishments.

An MP's job is long and exhausting. Over-indulging in food and drink is the enemy of work. The Palace of Westminster is awash with alcohol in the fifteen bars and countless daily receptions.

Advice on alcohol is simple. Don't drink at Westminster. Dennis Skinner argues faultlessly that he never drank when he was on duty down the mines. Why drink on duty in Parliament? It is not a lonely vocation. There is a large and growing band of Westminster teetotallers. The drinkers soon understand and stop offering drinks.

Abstemious Members can still plunge into the full joys of social life by sipping non-alcoholic drinks or by joining in the full delights of après-Parliament activities outside, when the House rises.

There is always a good reason for drinking. After a bad day a consoling swig is essential to rebuild collapsed spirits. After a good day, a celebratory glass is a deserved reward for success. It would be churlish to refuse a drink on social occasions in the constituency at week ends.

ORDER, ORDER!

That means some alcohol every day – the certain path to softening of the brain, cirrhosis of the liver and political impotence. Westminster drinkers have the added peril of speaking in the Chamber. Alan Clark is one of the few who have admitted to doing it. He survived, but only just.

The ideal timetable for a happy eater MP is:

8.30 a.m. Breakfast of toast and tea in the Members Tea Room. The Tea Room is the cradle of the Parliamentary day. Here the newspapers are read, embryo plots hatched, minor exploratory skirmishes between the parties bred. The day's battle plans are sketched out.

1.30 p.m. Light lunch of salad and oily fish in tea room (or cafeteria if you have staff or visitors with you).

7.30 p.m. Once or twice a week reward yourself with a deluxe three course dinner in the Members' Dining room. Avoid the same company, shuffle companions for quality conversation. Other nights, suffer the penance of character building two course meals in the cafeteria.

11.30 p.m. A cup of cocoa or decaffeinated coffee in bed listening to *Today in Parliament*.

Annie's Bar is a relic, a once famed meeting place of minds and hacks and MPs. Smart restaurants outside of the Palace are the new venues for plotting and leaking. The atmosphere of Annie's Bar now is one of comatose decrepitude – warriors raking over the ashes of fires that are long dead.

Bellamy's Bar is located in the swish, shining Parliament Street building. Heavily infested with researchers (mostly American), commanding view of Big Ben.

Bellamy's Restaurant and Clubroom. Cafeteria of good quality and value cursed by a troublesome plastic money system. Spooky clubroom with dominant paintings of a leprous Harold Wilson and a malevolent Thatcher upset digestion.

Churchill Room. Sumptuous and most expensive food. Stuffed with foreign visitors and celebrities.

Lords Bar. Most accessible bar open to unaccompanied staff. Psychedelic wallpaper. Menacing. Some of the inhabitants have been recruited by Hammer Horror Films casting.

Members' Dining Room/ Strangers. Now interchangeable they are served by one kitchen. Friendly staff, consistently good quality food. Now lived down its bad past when Ann Clwyd found a toe nail in a meal, and mice appeared at the window sills late in the evening.

Members Smoking Room. Mélange of Gentleman's Club and geriatric residential home. Refuge for alcohol addicts. Whisky-stained air. Someone could die in the plush chairs and not be noticed for days.

Members' Tea Room. Separated into party territories with a Welsh/ Ulster buffer zone in the middle. Exclusive to Parliamentarians it is the most popular venue for all, used by most MPs two or three times a day. Gossip epicentre of Parliament's village life. Prime Ministers drop in when they are in trouble. Universally loathed recent refurbishment with marble slabs provides warmth of an Italian funeral parlour.

Millbank Room. Veggie fare, little known fine bijou balcony for summer views, frequented by those with a small circle of friends. Book in advance for Fridays when researchers gorge there, taking advantage because the MP cats are away in their constituencies.

Portcullis Cafeteria at Millbank. Made-to-order sandwiches, high tables useful for the vertically challenged.

Pugin Room. Sinfully comfortable for pre-meal drinks, great view of Thames from window seat. Champagne-rich atmosphere. Popular for the lechers planning serious seduction, the religious plotting holy campaigns and for fat cat stroking. Best for celebrations, splendid multi-cultural staff.

Sports and Social. Newt-congenial ambience, down at heel low-life pub, entry is through Central Lobby reminiscent of a 'Speakeasy'. Democratic clientele from all sectors of village life. Hostile to intelligent quiet discussions.

Strangers' Bar. For unknown reasons a popular drinking hole, a remodelled corridor without charm. Low ceiling concentrates toxic air, breathing is as dangerous as car exhaust sucking. No regular customers live to the age of sixty. Crudest and most persistent lechers in the House. Regulars kiss each other a lot. Becomes tolerable in the summer with transfusions of fresh air and access to the river Terrace.

Terrace Cafeteria. Newly re-tiled, high quality pleasant cafeteria refurbished at huge cost. Extends to the outside embankment in the summer for Parliament's greatest delight, tea on the Terrace. Rightly loved by visitors and villagers.

Westminster Hall Cafeteria. Only to be used when other eating places are closed. Known as 'Fat Cops', it is attractive as a dining area only to anorectics. Interior is a replica of a nuclear fallout bunker.

How to be Comforted

The comfort stations at Westminster dominate many of the place's anecdotes, ancient and modern.

Women MPs had few until recently. There is now greater equality. A major concession was changing the signs on the men's loos from 'Members Only' to 'Male Members Only'. Also inviting ribaldry, the Lords are still called 'Peers Only'.

However, equality has not provided women members with anywhere as opulent as the Members' Cloak Room above the Cloisters. Hardly changed since Asquith or Churchill popped in. The stalls and basins are a minor triumph of Victorian marble and earthenware art. Someone should slap a preservation order on them. The airy opulence is redolent of an exclusive Gentleman's Club, complete with individual hand towels, combs and clothes brushes.

There is a room for the exclusive use of women Members, opposite the Smoking Room. There are comfortable furnished refuges from all persuasive maleness of the palace.

The Family Room, off the lower lobby, is a useful but inadequate crèche for the children and a refuge for the spouses of MPs who fail to get tickets for Question Time. It is comfortably furnished with settees, armchairs, a changing room plus an array of children's books.

The Party

How to be Whipped

The nature of the party Whips has been metamorphosised in the late nineties.

They swirl round in a never-never world of smiles, illusions, threats and whispers. Their name is taken from the hunting field where whips were used to goad the dim animals to do their masters' bidding.

Against the ambitious their power is boundless. Omnipresent Whips in the Chamber and Committees perpetually catalogue the strengths and weaknesses of Members' speeches. Their reports give novice MPs their first hoist up the greasy pole.

Their mission is to bind the party into compliant unity. Whips allocate offices, control pairing and hurl ashes on the heads of unorthodox members. No formal vows are demanded but their idea is to conjure up the peace, chastity and obedience of the monastic life. Except that to them poverty is not a virtue.

What Dennis Skinner called the 'organised truancy' of pairing collapsed in January 1997. The Whips' power was castrated. It soon became unbearable. The addicts returned to their old ways and pairing re-appeared in a slightly mutated form. There has been a gradual change. The tentacles of Whips' patronage have been losing their gripping power.

Pairing had long been the emergency balm spread to heal the wounds that the job inflicts on family life. Even the longest suffering spouses are outraged when family life is disrupted in order that the party can win or lose a division by fifty-eight votes rather than eight-five. The increasing influence of women MPs has lightened the burden of unreasonable hours. Members now boldly and rightly desert the Commons to shore up family life.

Newspapers delight in perpetuating the fantasy that whips discipline members with smarting 'raps across the knuckles'. Occasionally it is true for MPs whose pride is enfeebled by ambition. For the wise and self-respecting, a haranguing Whip is harangued back.

Expulsion

On the occasion when I almost reached the point of rupture from my party, discussion with the Whip was quiet and civilised. Only puny sanctions could be applied to a rarely pairing MP who had rejected the patronage of the whipping system. The direst threat was possible expulsion from membership of European Standing Committee B. During much of the previous year I had been my party's sole representative attending that desolate body.

Chief Whips know their only power is to swap a member's seat on an invisible committee for one in the studios of the vastly influential *Today* programme or *Newsnight*. Whipless MPs are no longer pariahs exiled to a forgotten world of silent solitude. They are welcomed and feted by the press, and their audiences and influence are hugely magnified.

The Whipless Tory Europhobes were immensely more powerful without their party's Whip. They disappeared back into obscurity when it was restored to them.

The Whips are powerless against substantial numbers of their flock. In every Parliament there are many whose ambition is dead, who have unassailable majorities or who are in their final term. Others have ideals and convictions that surmount personal ambition or the need to survive.

No discipline can be imposed on them. The only one that works is self discipline.

How to Befriend

Jerry Hayes tells me that the best advice he would offer a new MP is to develop friendships with a few MPs who can be implicitly trusted.

The waters of the Parliamentary world are infested with the sharks of competitiveness, malice and envy. A circle of close friends is the great survival buoyancy aid.

Some Members bond like swans for their entire Parliamentary

lives. Small groups of the same MPs are seen eating, debating and drinking together. Some friendships are enforced by party loyalty or geography, others by subject interests. School links are still strong between Tories although few want to dine in the company of their 'school fag' or the sixth former who bullied them.

MPs with shared interests flock together. The value is not merely social but a defence mechanism against hostile a Commons community who do not share the same enthusiasms.

There is practical value in having a list of colleagues who will allow their names to be added to EDMs and Motions without a prior say-so. They can come to the rescue when the member is double booked, short of passes to the Chamber or to swell an audience for a visiting dignitary. Vital are the voices that tell the truth when friends make fools of themselves

Avoid being trapped in ghettos of people with identical mind-sets to your own. Getting elected provides the admission ticket to some of the best informed and most stimulating company of any village in the country. Don't stick with those who shrink the boundaries of Parliamentary life.

How to Grow a Shell Back

Parliament is not a place for susceptible souls.

Sharp wounding attacks will come from all quarters. Most full-time politicians soon grow a shell back. Those barbs that penetrate deeply are the rare criticisms that are true or that come from friends.

Some MPs are shaken to the roots of their being by a whiff of critical comment. Depression sets in for long periods especially after a clever insult delivered in a Parliamentary sketch in papers read by MPs. Matthew Parris and Simon Hoggart of the *Times* and *Guardian* are the two most feared scourges. A verbal lashing or even a sneering adjective throws members with insecure egos into early morning gloom.

There is resilience to jibes of incompetence, immorality, bias or political incorrectness. Grief is experienced when an MP's personal appearance is mocked. An accusation that one front-bencher looks like a serial axe killer prompted recourse to the lawyers. A gibe challenged is usually a gibe doubled. Complaints rarely do any good, but give wider currency to the original insult.

Not many goals are scored from defensive positions. Attacks are best mounted from selected forward positions. Adjectives should be sharpened for an incisive retort and stored in an armoury of insults.

The ones who bounce back quickly from toe-curling revelations about their private lives are those who tough it out. Many have appeared in the Commons and deliberately asked Oral Questions hours after the publication of lurid accounts of shaming events in their private lives. In a recent case the disgraced MP told me he refused to read his old love letters printed by a tabloid. Self-induced amnesia was an effective antidote. The scandal was ephemeral.

However, the tormenting of Michael Fabricant by Simon Hoggart is eternal. The relationship between the two has become a minor parasitic industry. Is candidate Fabricant sponsored by Hoggart Enterprises plc? Has the *Guardian* shares in the future volume *Fabb, The Twilight Years*? Who is the host and who is the parasite? Who is feeding off whom? Hoggart has revealed that his name is an adopted one. Is he a closet Fabricant? Are they twins? Will we ever know the truth?

The Media

How to Handle the Press

These are the guaranteed ways of gaining publicity if you are a devotee of the discredited canard that all publicity is good for you:

* Make a total public prat of yourself.
* Echo popular base bigotry and prejudice.
* Attack a loved national institution, elderly royalty, cricket, a national hero.
* Marry someone 40 years your junior/ senior.
* Get kidnapped/ arrested/ shot at/ publicly drunk abroad.
* Attack your own party.
* Die in mysterious circumstances (preferably involving sex).

Dealing with tabloid journalists is like wrestling with cobras. They all have cruel small eyes and twisted mouths. Their trade is treachery. Cultivate a permanent state of trembling fear in their presence. Keep a witness at hand and never expect 'off the record' pleas to be respected. After long and bitter experience, Tony Benn records all his conversations with them.

Their stories are dominated by the political priority of their proprietors and editors and only marginally influenced by the facts.

Broadsheet journalists follow the theme of the day. By a process of osmosis they jointly decide the issue and the line of the moment. The process is irrational, driven by herd and lem-

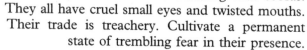

BUT THAT'S CONTRARY TO WHAT YOU SAID TO YOUR WIFE OVER BREAKFAST ON MONDAY

ming instincts. The motive is self-protection. Brilliantly they all reach the same conclusion. Nobody is left out. Nobody is wrong. If the conclusion of the day suits you, babble away. If not, don't waste time. They will not be convinced that there is an alternative truth.

Local journalists need the local MP. The Member needs them in an inverse ratio to the size of the majority. The best relationship is founded on common trust and respect. Worth working for on both sides. Recently many quality local papers have plunged down market. Their tabloid front pages repeatedly carry harrowing pictures of dying children, scarred crime victims or nuns with cheques for a bleeding heart cause.

Some new regional journalists are reared in special veal crates in an alien land. Their restricted diet contains no nutrition for brain development. Tailor your press statement to appeal to their new tabloid standards. One hack relates how his eye witness story of the start of the Gulf War was interrupted by a request from the news editor of a south Wales paper 'Not bad Mike, but what is the connection with Glamorgan?'

The demands of the electronic media are all embracing. MPs should strive to do interviews on their terms. Be grateful when 5% of the listeners or viewers get the message. They all will notice if you are out of breath, or have untidy or dishevelled hair or a twisted tie or dress. There is no time to be professionally made up for all Westminster interviews. The well organised modern MP of either sex packs a handy make-up kit.

Drag adverse criticism of media performances from friends. Irritating voices, constant repetitions of meaningless expressions, distracting gestures must be identified and corrected. Trade Minister Jonathan Evans in a brief interview on *Newsnight* in September 1995 used the vacuity 'In point of fact', to bridge the gaps between his thoughts six times. It was hypnotic stuff. The nation, deaf to his message, waited for the seventh boot to drop.

I was further educated in media relations when I employed a researcher who had previously worked for megastar Tony Banks. Unexpectedly, I was in great demand on a Tuesday morning. In commanding style she marshalled the interview slots. She bullied the press to do her bidding to get maximum coverage for the campaign message. 'If you want an interview you must bring a crew up to Westminster,' she told BBC *Breakfast Time.* 'No, he cannot possibly come down to White City. If you want him that's what you have to do. There was no trouble fixing things with GMTV.' It worked. A crew and live link were sent at the peak viewing time of 8.10 a.m. as demanded.

That episode almost washed from my memory a day ruined by an inexperienced researcher. She booked me a rambling interview with an obscure Hospital Radio. Many of the maximum of one hundred listeners were asleep, too infirm to remove their headphones or dead. The following day she said that someone else wanted an interview. Compassionately she had given precedence to the radio, 'I think the other one's name was Jon Snow, from a television programme.'

Lacing humour with a serious subject can be ruinous. A joke by Labour's spokeswoman on women, Janet Anderson, that women would be more promiscuous 'under Labour' went nuclear. In a tedious hour long interview in Welsh about drugs I said that magic mushrooms could be legally cultivated and exported when fresh, but became a class A drug if stored overnight. The comment was never broadcast but was press released a month later by the producers to suggest I was advocating new drug exporting entrepreneurs. Understandably the media were hooked.

How to Write for the Papers

The *Votingham Gazette* may well appreciate a regular column. It is a very useful conduit to the constituents but secondary to other media.

It does not always work. Nicholas Bennett (Pembroke, 1983-87) wrote probably a record four weekly columns for constituency newspapers. Nevertheless, he lost his seat with a huge swing against him. His electronic media persona incited anxiety in his constituents.

Insist on payment, even a microscopic one. Otherwise bread is taken out of the mouths of underpaid local hacks. Personal tax must be paid on fees. The rest should be channelled into a local charity or a fund for charitable donations. The cash must be declared in the Members' Interest Book. Pocketing it is not worth the resentment aroused. It is helpful to explain that there is no personal profit from the articles.

Select a readable formula. Avoid a slab of words. Work on the assumption that all newspapers readers read the headlines but one per cent only read the thousand word features. Divide the contribution into word morsels of minimum length. Four or five shorts items of less than one hundred and fifty words are perfect.

Insist on an attractive format on a well read page. Push for illustrations and write with an eye for opportunities for photographs. The Commons supplies dozens of chances for newsworthy picture every week. Even a decent picture of a visiting school party or pensioners' group is newsworthy in Votingham.

A weekly diet of party political diatribe will be as unwelcome to the editor as it will be indigestible to the readers. Confine columns to a maximum of a fifth hard political argument. The bulk of the pieces should be irresistible tasters of Parliamentary gossip, jokes, consumer items and Votingham events.

Rarely is it worthwhile to write speculatively for the national press. Nearly all articles are pre-arranged with the features editor. If an idea for a feature is rejected, it is sensible to accept an offer to print a letter instead. The letters pages are well read.

Papers with political agendas court MPs who are at odds with their parties. The *Daily Express* and the *Sun* invited me to write articles on education in 1996. Never before had they shown even a vestigial interest in any of my views. They both refused to give me any control of cuts in the article or of the illustrations, pictures or headlines that would accompany it. They could and almost certainly would have distorted my words by their presentation into an attack on my party.

The *Sunday Times* has repeatedly trapped the innocent or Parliamentary wannabes into writing self-damaging articles. Their technique is to persuade someone on the right or left extremes of the parties to write something outrageous. MPs on the opposite wing are invited to be provoked. The paper then has an article inside and a front page story on a New Party Split. Some recent pieces have been placed after being written by anonymous researchers, then topped and tailed with a sentence from a would-be rising star.

For three successive Saturdays, Andrew Grice, the chief political hack at the *Sunday Times* invited me to rage against pieces on Labour 'no longer socialist', and 'no longer taxing the rich'. I declined to give them a spilt story. Others did not.

A variation in January 1996 was an invitation for me to write an article on Midwitch Socialists. It was a 'Fable for our Times' that I had previously described in a column in the Welsh language magazine *Golwg*. They sent a former editor of the Insight feature to Parliament to persuade me. I asked whether they would contact Labour's spin doctors on the day before publication and invite them to denounce me and my fable. His dumb response confirmed that the *Sunday Times* were playing the same game. Beware.

Usually the role is reversed and MPs are seeking outlets for articles. Hundreds of specialist magazines are readily accessible markets for campaigning material. They should not be neglected.

The painful labour of creative writing is never wasted. There is no better method of organising thoughts. Unpublished tracts can be recycled as questions, letters and speeches.

How to Broadcast

Availability is the key to success. Pagers that silently vibrate and alert have now become essential. The instant needs of broadcasters are met when they can lassoo the meandering Member anywhere.

In answer to the increasing defensive and evasive skills of politicians, interviewers have grown more aggressive. Try a trial interview with a friend beforehand, preferably one with journalistic skills. Explore the weaknesses in your case and prepare defences.

Ask how long your broadcast contribution is expected to be. Divide the answer by three. Pack your message into the resulting number of seconds. Ten seconds of a quietly delivered sentence in which every word glows will hit the spot. A whole minute of rushed garbled generalities will miss the target.

Number Four Millbank is now the temple of Parliament's electronic media. It spreads itself into the adjoining green areas when weather permits.

The time values for electronic media:

15 secs on main television news bulletin =
40 secs on the Radio 4 *Today* programme =
3 mins on *Newsnight* =
10 mins on networked BBC / IRN local radios =
30 mins on Radio Five Live =
60 mins on single regional television station =
One and half hours on Talk Radio/ Radio One =
Six months on single local radio =
2 eternities on Votingham Hospital Radio

Try to do the least important interview first. Your message will sharpen with each interview.

How to Bargain Fees

Don't, except where MPs' work displaces that of hacks. The media is the binding force between the Member and the constituents. In a modern democracy it is essential that they the link is close and constant. The now popular haggling over fees implies that MPs refuse to perform if the fee is too low. There may be justification for this in entertainment shows. For news and information programmes, MPs should not seek to profit for performing a crucial part of the job for which they have already been paid.

Those who argue that MPs pay needs to be supplemented are often the same ones that vote against any salary increases. MPs have the means to set their own wage. Back door bargaining demeans the status of Parliamentarians and is an impediment to open communication. What is legitimate is payment of small 'disturbance' fees for out of pocket expenses, and fees for items where scripts need to be prepared.

Politicians do tout for cash. When I took part in Channel Four's *The Great Pot Debate* one of the MPs on the panel of four Parliamentarians told me that he had refused to appear without a fee of £100. 'You'll all be getting the same – thanks to me,' he boasted.

Andrew Roth reported (*New Statesman* 8th September 1995)

that John Biffen's secretary had demanded £160 for two broadcasts by John on LBC in 1992. Roth quotes her as saying that 'he only undertakes interviews for payment and certainly the BBC, ITV and Sky do pay up.' That may explain why John is now rarely seen on the box.

BBC fees are often immutable. From 1986 to 1994 I took part in a BBC Radio Wales programme called *The Critics*. A fee was sensible. A few hours work was involved in researching three subjects and preparing a script. For eight years the fee remained the same at £44. Now 'producer choice' means that BBC rarely pay fees at all for news items and small amounts when preparatory work has to be done by the interviewee.

A reliable gauge is the bigger the audience the smaller the fee. Radio Four's *Today* programme is top for influence and pays nothing. No fee is paid for the *Jimmy Young Show* or the main television bulletins.

How to Dress

Unobtrusively for males. Your clothes should not upstage your words. The most dramatic illustration of clothing eclipsing a speech occurred with one of Parliament's most sober dressers.

Toby Jessel is a strictly three piece suit man and frequently wears a tie with red and green diagonal stripes. It looks like a regimental or an old school tie. His usual dress fault is that his stomach swells to expose a white shirt midriff between his waistcoat and the top of his trousers.

That is nothing compared to his day of sartorial ignominy. His speeches are delivered in an excited red faced bluster. But it was not his face that riveted the attention of the television audience.

The voice-over commentator in hushed tones explained that the speaker was 'Toby Jessel, Conservative, Twickenham'. A few moments later the commentator found it necessary to explain that the object poking out of the flies of Mr Jessel's trousers was the end of his tie.

Some of the viewers had never seen a red and green one before.

It was red ties that were recommended with blue suits when the cameras first appeared in the House. Led by Eric Forth and Austin Mitchell, ties have blossomed into an orgy of wild clashing colours. Eric's have included a flash of lightning and a psychedelic exploding tomato. Austin peaks with national flags and a *Baywatch* special. When either speaks there is murmur of interest. The ties are the topic, not the speeches. The House is far more interested in the flag of Borneo or the artist's wipe rag around their necks.

Dennis Canavan intrigued the House with an oddly cut suit that married the styles of Armani and the Nicaragua Sandinistas. It was the current uniform used by urban guerrilla warriors. Two stubbornly proletarian jackets have been used for years by Dennis Skinner and Rhodri Morgan. Rhodri has now wilted under criticism and dumped his mud-spattered effect tweed. Dennis is soldiering on with the longest surviving garment in the Chamber. It has become a symbol of unchanging working class solidarity.

Women MPs raise little excitement even when their colours are audacious and startling. Elizabeth Peacock regularly wears Welsh national costume minus the hat. Edwina Currie once sported a heavily shoulder-padded yellow costume indistinguishable from surplus Rumanian Securitate uniforms that were on sale in downtown Bucharest at the time. Teresa Gorman has a yellow and black costume – nature's danger signals. Did this subliminally inspire her nickname of 'Jewelled Wasp'?

How to Say No to the Media

The agendas of hacks and MPs often overlap. But they are still separate. So demanding of the time of MPs is the media that it can seriously detract from the work of a Member. Important as they are, their interests are subservient to those of constituents.

The late John Stradling-Thomas was an affable raconteur who found life as a Minister difficult after happy years as a Whip: 'I like to kick arse, not to have mine kicked'. As a senior MP he had a long relationship of trust with journalists. He gave an interview to a tabloid hack and entertained him in a Commons bar. At one point the room emptied, then filled up again fifteen minutes later. John explained that they had been to hear Prime Minister's Question Time but that he did not bother any more. The journalist wrote a piece under the heading of 'Britain's laziest MP'.

There were many other MPs who were far more deserving of that epithet than Stradling-Thomas. But he made the mistake of saying 'yes' and dropping his guard. His career and life of considerable service ended ignominiously.

The political agendas of many papers send hacks scurrying in search of damaging quotes from garrulous politicians or those who are off guard. Their techniques are usually crude and obvious.

Some journalists expect MPs offices to do their research for them. Without a blush they ask for information that might take hours to assemble. Frequently there is little or no advantage for the Members or current campaigns. Junior researchers on television programmes are the most demanding and time wasting.

The Constituency

How to Please Constituents

MPs should bond closely with their constituents. The relationship is that of a priest and parishioners, solicitor and clients, shepherd and flock. The MP should be the living embodiment of the constituency, tirelessly promoting and defending the patch with the ferocity of a mother protecting her offspring.

A modern MP must be a creature of the local habitat. Only by living, shopping, sharing local schools and entertainment can the Member fulfil the increasingly vital task as the constituency's ambassador to the centres of powers.

Expectations of what an MP can do vary widely. Some constituents write on a weekly basis with their latest thoughts. Others apologetically ring once a decade on matters of life and death. Happily the great majority are reasonable and are satisfied if the Member has tried to help even if there are no satisfactory results.

Confidence is built slowly between MP and constituents. Hacks are constantly seeking examples from Members' casebooks to illustrate their stories. Any personal matter raised by a constituent should be protected with the secrecy of the confessional.

How to Hide the Address

Most MPs now live in their constituencies. Concealing a home address is entirely legitimate. Even MPs are entitled to reasonable privacy. Their families certainly are. If the address is well known, constituents will call in at any hour of the day. It is not much fun when the neighbourhood arsonist, rapist or a weirdo drops in for a chat late at night. Even less amusing is when the call occurs during the week when the MP is in London and the spouse or kids are home alone.

Complaining constituents are often angry and violent, as Benefits Agency staff testify by insisting on grills and anonymous name badges. One woman brought her six foot gorilla of a boyfriend to my home and explained to my wife that he had been falsely accused of rape 'again'.

If the home address is well known before the election, there is one choice only – move. Then never tell anyone the new address. Almost daily there will be requests for details of the new home. Many are from people late sending mail trying to steal an extra day. Always refuse.

There is a serious security risk. MPs are still liable to receive letter bombs from a range of zealots. At Westminster mail is screened. If the new address becomes known, divert all your letters to Westminster. Even during the recess there need be no delay because urgent mail can be faxed by staff.

The only occasion where there is a legal obligation to publish your address is on the nomination forms for your election. It is legitimate to use your London address or your party office in the constituency to circumvent this.

How to Convince Voters that the MP Never Stops Working

Never stop working.

The alternative is to organise the day to give the impression of a perpetually-working MP. Offices should be organised to respond immediately to letters and phone calls. Backlogs should be cleared with overtime and no self respecting MP's office has a pending tray.

Modern technology amplifies MP's work. One letter to the readers' letter page of the *Votingham Argus* can be effort-lessly reproduced and sent to hundreds of other papers through the wonders of a database. Constituents with specialised con-cerns can be clustered into computer nests that can be called up instantly for an update letter on their subject.

Be ubiquitous and ever present in the constituency. The drip feed of press releases, early morning radio interviews that are repeated throughout the day, widely advertised surgeries and attendance in the Chamber in a camera-exposed position, all propagate the message 'Busy MP'.

Some skilled Gullivers are adept at organising staff to fax their views to papers while they are sunning themselves and finding heaps of new facts in a sun kissed exotic foreign location.

How to Soothe the Constituents

The telephone number and the House of Commons address should be the only contact points for constituents. 'Drop in' offices for complaints help nobody. They attract swarms of complaints that cannot be dealt with by MPs. Inevitably they disappoint those who need help from the Citizens Advice Bureau, Council Office or The Samaritans. So overwhelmed did one high profile MP's town centre constituency office become, the staff lost control and complaints were delayed for months or lost.

Surgeries should be either first come, first served or by appointment. Some have attempted to mix the two and have had fist fights in their waiting rooms. Surgeries without appointment are inefficient and waste the time of MPs and constituents. Only one in ten attending have complaints that can be usefully tackled. An appointment system will limit surgery attenders to those with serious problems that need a long discussion or an examination of documents.

Others who ring or write can have immediate action on their worries. Many are usefully advised to re-direct their complaints to a body that can help. A surprising number contact MPs outside of their areas and have to be diverted to their own MP.

The expectation is growing of the omnipotence of MPs as the point of help of last resort. Complaints vary. A woman rang me from a hotel in Milan to say her husband had died ten minutes ago and asked what should she do next. I was paged in the Chamber by a man who complained that the dustman had left his emptied bin in the middle of his drive. He had been forced to stop his car and move the bin to the side. I asked why he was ringing me. He said he had already rung 10 Downing Street and they told him to contact me.

On the same morning I had a call from a woman whose husband was about to be deported to his certain death in an African country. Shortly before a man complained that he had fitted four new tyres on his car and one of them had worn quicker than the others. All parts of the warp and weave of Parliamentary life.

Unwanted publicity exacerbates constituents' problems with wounding attention to private matters. Occasionally it helps. Any delayed hospital operation or appointment will be expedited following publicity in the local paper. Never allow journalists details of contact numbers of constituents without first getting their permission.

How to Say No

Even the most devoted Member has to reject requests. Otherwise campaigners, the obsessed, third parties and students will swamp the work of the office and make it unmanageable.

The limited role of the two- or three- person MP's team must be established with outside groups who share campaign objectives. Productive relations will collapse if either make unreasonable demands on the other.

A tiny number of constituents and campaigners can hi-jack the attention of the office with a relentless flow of letters and phone calls. Often they have genuine grievances or are pushing fine causes. Sooner rather than later they must be told firmly that they are destroying goodwill and exasperating staff. They have a single all-consuming problem and fail to understand the mass of daily demands on a MP's time.

Only accept complaints from third parties for reason of disability or language interpretation. Solicitors, agents in ethnic communities and relatives must be told that constituents must contact the MP directly. Tell them that information received second-hand is often inaccurate and incomplete. Some third parties charge for passing cases on. Services provided by an MP must not be subject to a charge of any kind. Provide details of the Commons address and telephone numbers.

The demands of students for interviews, articles and information are now insatiable. Some ring for a half an hour chat in the middle of a fraught day. Others expect their essays or theses to be written for them. They send a lists of questions that would take a couple of hours to answer. A practical policy is to try to answer fully 'seed corn' constituency students and those sympathetic to current campaigns. Articles and *Hansard* debates should be mass photocopied and filed in anticipation. They can be easily dispatched.

There is no hope of dealing with non-constituent general inquiries on unfamiliar or exotic subjects. Say so.

More difficult is refusing invitations which say, 'You've been babbling about it. Come up and see for yourself.' After I had an adjournment debate about the increasing numbers of hip operations that went wrong, a surgeon from Wigan, Mr Wroblewski, invited me to visit. The planned programme was:

9.30 a.m. Watch a hip replacement operation.
11.30 a.m. Watch a revision operation.
1.30 p.m. Lunch.

Lunch? After that lot! Pressure of work forced me to unselfishly delegate the trip to a researcher.

Blackmailing charity invitations are the most difficult to turn down. 'Well, what would you have done?' John Marshall asked me, 'if they say they would give £200 to your favourite charity to do it?' when I pulled his leg about a picture of him. 'Reach for your cheque book, John,' I suggested.

That morning there was a glorious photograph of John on the front page of the *Independent*. He was wearing a sunflower hat, a flower patterned hooped dress, carrying a parasol and holding a lead attached to a sheep named Gwendolyn. The deal was cash for charity if John dressed up as Bo Beep and walked across Tower Bridge with Gwendolyn. MPs can make fools of themselves without the help of outside bodies. It is not part of the job to be a hired clown even for good causes.

How to Be a Conduit

A central task is to be the channel through which the fears and hopes of all groups in the constituency are directed to Government.

Industry, the NHS, the Police, charitable bodies, community groups, all rightly claim that their cases must be heard at the top level. There is no discretion. Their best interests must be served.

Every sizable organisation deserves at least one visit per Parliament. The resulting detailed knowledge is essential. Mutual trust and confidence should be built. The products of local firms must be vigorously promoted in every Parliamentary arena. Local life should be celebrated. Most success owes a great deal to hype. All facets of life in Votingham from local charities, local government successes, pop groups, innovative products, tourist locations, any aspect of local life of quality or distinction must be shamelessly and tirelessly sold.

The conduit must be wide open for immediate two way contact with telephones and fax messages, to deal with unexpected events.

How to Find the Silent Voices

A widespread delusion of many MPs is that the concerns of constituents are fairly represented in messages received or day to day contacts. They are not.

MPs resent being told that they should 'get out more and meet ordinary people'. Aren't they always out meeting everybody? Yes, but they far more likely to meet the police chief than a constable, or to be on buddy terms with the editor of a local paper rather than his van drivers or paper sellers. The chair of the NHS Trust writes regularly but no word from a hospital cleaner. Meals are in the directors' suite rather than the works canteen. Seductively, the single Patrician dominates our thoughts to the exclusion of the hundred Plebeians.

Never visit a school, police station or business without talking to the canteen workers, the cleaners and the caretaker. They deserve more time than the headteacher, the managing director or the chief of police. Those who write, phone or attend surgeries are predominantly the well informed, the articulate or the fanatics. Silent are the voices of the fearful, the downcast, or the illiterate.

A million pensioners in Britain do not take up the income support that is their due because of ignorance of the system. They are weakly motivated. They are also ones who never contact their MPs.

It essential to undertake a rigorous regular stocktake of office priorities. Has a disproportionate amount of the time and energy of the MP and team been hijacked, bullied or pressurised into wrong directions? Has reacting to invitations, requests and media demands distorted the workload to the detriment of those in greatest need of an MP's work? Has the value of the activity advanced or retreated because of hostility from vested interests, the media or cowardice?

Falling into a re-active routine enfeebles and demoralises the work of members and staff. Ideals must be re-discovered. New contacts initiated. Ideas refreshed and invigorated. Shock therapy must jump start the paralysis of routine.

Writing this on the morning of 5th February 1997 I received an invitation to a luxury, champagne-drenched bash from lobbyists for British Airways. Today's headline in the *Western Mail* is about abused children in a residential home. They said: 'We didn't know who to complain to.'

How to Sympathise

A highly successful councillor in my constituency, Jim Kirkwood, was taken to task by a constituent. He said that his vote was going elsewhere. The reason was unexpected. 'You didn't come to my father's funeral,' the constituent complained. Jim expressed his sympathy and asked whether he knew the deceased. 'No, you didn't know him but neither did the other candidate. But he turned up at the funeral.' Jim was perplexed. Is he expected to haunt funerals with feigned regret at the deaths of complete strangers? Jim did not change his tactics. He was elected. His opponent lost.

In 1962 I received a message of congratulation on my marriage from the late Raymond Gower, then MP for Barry. He was renowned as a diligent constituency MP with a large personal vote. By today's standards the message was woeful. It was a crude Gestetnered pro-forma offering 'Congratulations on your birthday/ anniversary/ birth of the baby/ marriage/ examination success.' The MP had made the appropriate deletions and signed the form.

The information had been taken from the 'Hatched, Matched and Dispatched' pages of the local paper. He had an alternative pro-forma expressing sympathy for bereavement. The process was universal and poorly targeted. The evidence is that these notes worked. Raymond Gower's personal vote was genuine and large. Similar tactics now would be mocked as amateurish. They are also accident prone. Lists of ex-patients from local hospitals were sent 'Get well soon letters'. Some had been in for abortions that they wanted to keep quiet. Others had died.

Nevertheless, when sympathy is heartfelt MPs should pass on their thoughts. Sincerity will shine through, especially with a hand written message. When the family or the deceased is known personally great pains should be taken writing an individual letter. It is an important part of the job and can also aid the healing process for the bereaved.

When other terrible events occur that have a political dimension, deference and restraint must be paramount. The relatives should be approached, if at all, with care and tenderness. Those MPs who leap to wring political advantage from tragedy are the vultures of Westminster.

How to Nourish the Seed Corn

For unfathomable reasons loyalty is given at a tender age to favourite football teams, pop stars and political parties. Often the devotion is life-long. Part of the job is to ensure that Votingham fledglings are attracted to the correct causes.

Schools welcome visits from the local Member. Least useful is a booming stage presence at prize day, spraying pompous pieties to resentful fidgeting audiences. To clear the conduit of information from student to MP and back again, there must be an exchange of ideas.

Vocabulary is a prime obstacle. The difference between primary school talk and House of Commons talk is comparable to the gulf between Oxford English and Rap. Big variations in language and understanding exist even between year groups.

THEN I SAY, OH NO IT ISN'T AND YOU SAY, OH YES IT IS!

The only hope of connecting with the kids is to induce them to talk freely. Then try to join in on their wavelength. A good format is to play House of Commons. Find out what issues divide them. Which pop group is best? Is fox hunting O.K.? Should animal experimenters be executed? Should polluters be jailed?

Select a talkative advocate for and against and set up a mini debate. The MP grabs the theatrical role by acting as Speaker and booming 'Order, Order' frequently. The pantomime of baying and grunting in Commons style and not clapping is quickly learned and enjoyed.

Table a simple motion, allow a free debate from the class after the main speakers. Insist on a vote. This is a fine lesson in democracy plus the chance of dropping embryonic political truths. The kids love it. A benign message is taken home to the voting parents.

Teachers enjoy sending painstakingly prepared letters and pictures from every member of a class. Encourage it as a useful channel of information. They are glorious campaigning and heart winning opportunities. Devote a few hours to write fully tailored replies to each letter. They will be joyously received and read many times by parents and relatives.

The seed corn is prepared for a future harvest.

How to Switch On Young Voters

To most young people MPs are cynical, rich, antique lechers who hail from the planet Zog. MTV-saturated young people have long had their brains marinaded in rock music. They know politics is a hideous novocaine for the senses delivered in an alien tongue.

The gulf between the generations is as unbridgeable as ever. The most absurd politicians are those who preach to the young

on the evils of today's drug culture. From any of the fifteen
bars in the Commons, sexage-
narian MPs can be witnessed
denouncing the evils of drug
use while holding a whisky in
one hand, a cigarette in the
other and a couple of paraceta-
mol in their pocket for their
daily headache.

Few have ever tried to penetrate the youth culture that
often revolves around drugs.
Most youngsters are extremely
well informed on the character
of illegal drugs. They know

SO, APART FROM A RUNNING JUMP,
WHAT *ELSE* CAN WE POLITICIANS
DO FOR YOUNG PEOPLE LIKE YOU?

that many are less toxic and addictive than the legal drugs consumed on an orgiastic scale in the Palace of Westminster.

Intelligent communication between MPs and young people is
possible only after mind twisting adjustments. MPs first have to
undergo disturbing questioning of their own mental omnipotence before alien youthful ideas can be understood.

Local pop culture can by usefully hyped through the
Westminster publicity megaphone. If it is a promising source of
local jobs and pride, the MPs should promote it. It is unwise and
dangerous to affect an implausible liking for contemporary
music or mores. Sergeant Bilko lookalike, balding Michael
Neubert told Parliament that that he swapped places with his
daughter for a day. She worked as the MP. He pranced and
yelped as a disc jockey at the local rock club. It's hard to imag-
ine a less convincing DJ.

David Mellor has been successful though his Radio 5 football
show in winning popularity from young people. Enthusiasm for
animal welfare is still strong among teenagers, but environmental concerns have lost many of their followers in the past ten
years. Yet these are still the strongest contacts across the gener-
ation chasm.

Middle-aged and elderly MPs should cauterise their nerve
endings and witness some youth culture. Without patronising,

middle-aged MPs can show they know the difference between Mark Lamar and Heddy Lamar, *Shooting Stars* and shooting up, or Pterodactyl and Terrorvision.

How to Run a Rough Tour

For the coach parties of visitors from Votingham to Parliament, facilities are a disgrace. For the rich, articulate and privileged, the welcome is sumptuous. But for the coaches of constituency groups, often pensioners and school children, the visit to their Parliament is a once in a lifetime treat. The system neglects them. Only very recently have they been sheltered from the weather in the queue outside. Toilet facilities are inadequate. Large parties cannot visit the Terrace, nor have the simple hospitality of a welcoming cup of tea.

In spite of all, a visit is a wonderful experience and greatly enjoyed. The job of the MP is to make things go smoothly. Prepare a letter to send to all inquirers to blow away some of the illusions and provide some practical advice.

It is a foolish under-use of the time, and more importantly the energy of an MP, to act routinely as a guide on a tour. The maximum allowed per guide, including MPs, is sixteen. Two thirds of a coach party of forty-eight will be antagonised when only a third of them have the joy of the five star guide spiel.

Sometimes because of cock-ups or with small parties, the MP or staff must take over. Don't repeat the common mistake of professional guides. They wake up sweating in the early hours of the morning worrying because they have forgotten an historical fact, or a date.

Parties of tired, foot sore constituents need the stimulus of jokes and excitement. Usually they are crushed down with slabs of incomprehensible, indigestible facts and dates.

Rough Guide, or The Only Bits People Remember

Welcome!
The proper name for this marvellous place is The Palace of Westminster. It is divided into three parts.
Up above this massive stone ceiling is the Victoria Tower. It

dominates the first part, the Royal Chambers. The middle part is the Lords and thirdly, the Commons. Remember the three parts. Royal, colour Gold; Lords, Red; Commons, Green. You'll notice when we pass from the Lords to the Commons, even the carpet changes colour.

Robing Room. We are following the footsteps of the Queen when she opens Parliament. This magnificent room has one purpose only. It is used once a year by the Queen to change her dress. All the interior was designed by Augustus Pugin. Everything. The ceilings, furniture, ash trays. He went completely mad and died at the age of forty.

Who can spot the Queen's lavatory? That's right! The door is hidden as part of the panelling in the top right hand corner of the room. You can see the door handle. The lozenges in the ceiling (that's really what they are called) have the initials VR on them. First evidence that Queen Victoria's Consort Albert chaired the committee responsible for the redecoration of the place after the fire in 1834. He seized every chance to give his wife a plug.

Gallery. This Royal Gallery is used as a corridor for the Queen when she is kitted out with all the procession. She walks down the middle here, with some simpleton in front of her walking backwards carrying a big key on a cushion. I believe he's called the Stick Carrier in Waiting.

The other purpose of the room is to embarrass foreign visitors. The two paintings are of Waterloo and Trafalgar. When President Mendes of France visited, he was received here. It was to rub his nose in the memories of our two British victories.

The artist Daniel Maclise had a bit of wife trouble when he was painting these huge pictures. 'Not off up to Westminster again tonight, with your old painting, leaving me on my own with kids.' To console her he painted her into the picture. She's the nurse. There's her name 'Polly' on the seal of the water pitcher.

All the gorgeous red and gold in the Lord's Chamber has grown even more gaudy over the years as their powers decline. A good rough guide to understanding this place is that the more glorious the decoration the chambers have, the less the power is wielded there.

THE CONSTITUENCY

When the Queen delivers the speech the Prime Minister has written for her, she, and her family and the Lords sit. Members of the Commons have to stand in that tiny sheep pen at the back. Things have become more democratic. At one time, when the monarch spoke, the Lords stood and members of the Commons had to kneel.

Those red curtains in front of the seats in the public gallery are recent. There were introduced when the twenties flappers wore short skirts. The noble lords could not concentrate enough to legislate. The view of all that bare flesh set off a few heart attacks among them.

Central Lobby. This is the centre of the building – the intersection of the cross, here in the middle of the Central Lobby. Behind us, you can see the red of the Queen's Throne in the Lords. In an exact straight line is the Green of the Speaker's chair in the Commons. Here everyone is entitled to come to 'lobby' their MP.

The best part of the Central Lobby is the ceiling. The quickest way of getting to know the place is by remembering the reason for the location of the pictures of the four saints.

St Patrick for Ireland is over the St Stephen's chapel which is the main exit from the building. He is there because the Irish have long been uncertain whether they want to stay in this Parliament. The English suffer from the delusion that they are better than every one else. So St George is positioned above the route to the Lords. St Andrew for Scotland is placed over the road to the Stranger's Bar, the Smoke Room (Bar) and the Peers Bar. St David (Dewi Sant) bestrides the line to the Commons Debating Chamber because all Welsh people speak so beautifully. It's only fair to tell you that there are other versions of this story.

Members' Lobby. The Members' Lobby is the forum of Parliament. When divisions are being held, it is full of hundreds of chattering MPs. During the day journalists and MPs group together, to gossip, plot and tell tales usually about other journalists and MPs. Anything said here is on lobby terms and its source must not be revealed.

The mark on the door is where Back Rod hits it after it is slammed in his face when he summons the MPs to 'attend the

Queen in the House of Peers'. In the attendant's box nearby is a shelf where a box of snuff is placed every day. In the last Parliament, only one member used it, the late Nicholas Fairbairn. The cost then was 87p a year to the exchequer. Now nobody uses it.

Commons Chamber. The first thing we see as we go into the Commons Chamber is this huge bag. Petitions are put in when the House is in session. Hence, the expression 'It's in the bag'. It is locked when visitors are going through because the attendants are tired of fishing out the crisp packets and chocolate wrappers passing visitors dump in it.

That huge spreading wooden canopy on top on the Speaker's Chair is no accident. The reason it is that shape is because there used to be a rail with curtains running around the chair. At that time there was only one Speaker, and he had to remain in the chair for very long periods. If he (and it was always 'he') was absent, the House was no longer is session.

The Speakers will tell you that the curtains were drawn across for privacy when the 'Speaker's Chop' was brought in. In those days he certainly needed to eat on the job. But the sight was unlikely to have distressed the members. They were not that fastidious. The real reason for drawing the curtains was so the Speaker could use the commode that was then built into the chair. On those occasions, it was customary to cheer.

Anyone crossing these two red lines in the carpet when speaking to the House, will be howled down with shouts of 'Order'. It's a nasty experience. The lines are two sword lengths plus one foot apart. They were necessary when Members were all armed with pig stickers. The green space in the middle is still the Parliamentary battlefield's no-persons-land.

The little dent on the Prime Minister's Dispatch Box was supposed to have been made by Winston Churchill – banging his fist down and knocking the wood with his ring. The same story is told about Asquith.

St Stephen's Hall. This was once a chapel. That is the reason MPs bow in the direction of the Speaker, even when she's not in the chair. They are bowing to the Blessed Sacrament that was kept in the same place in the chapel. The crack in the sword and the missing spur on the Falkland statue shows the damage caused releasing a suffragette who had chained herself to it.

Westminster Hall. This is the oldest and grandest part of the building. The walls were built nine hundred years ago. It was saved twice from fire while other parts of the palace were left burning.

Charles I was tried here. He suffered an extra cruelty at the trial when his spaniel lap dog was taken away from him. It was his comforter. Without it he stuttered. Charles II took his revenge by digging up Cromwell's body and displaying his head over the great North Door. It stayed there for eighteen years until it was blown down in a gale.

In the last century, a Fenian bomb was carried by a policeman from the crypt steps into the middle of the hall. It blew out the South window and made a crater in the floor. After the IRA bomb damaged the wooden roof in the seventies, workers discovered leather tennis balls in the beams. They are thought to have been lost by Henry VIII when he played royal tennis here.

How to See Off Challengers for the Seat

The country is full of would be MPs. It is possible to become neurotic about pretenders to that well stacked majority. In times of party decline in the polls, fellow MPs nervously plot chicken runs. Boundary changes destroy majorities and umbilical links with well served constituents.

It is unwise to expect local parties to act reasonably in their selections. Experience tells a tale of irrational choices. Faithful, talented, hard-working members have been ditched in favour of slothful rogues.

Working well and avoiding scandal are only the start of becoming superglued to the Parliamentary seat. The local party must be subjected to relentless wooing between elections. Last minute attempts to win over neglected, resentful constituents will be brushed off. Good works are not enough. The news must be immodestly and continuously conveyed to the Votingham party.

Every conceivable boundary change should be anticipated. Neighbouring constituency parties should be constantly cultivated as possible future inhabitants of redrawn constituency boundaries. Aspirant favourite daughters and sons in the constituency should be respected and never underestimated. Sitting Members have been cast into the wilderness as punishment for their delusions of permanence or adequacy.

One Tory association tried to give their venerable member a gentle heave-ho in 1986. In 1982 he had been selected with a narrow majority promising that it would be his last term. To cement the pledge the party held a valedictory dinner in his honour a full year before the next election.

It was a sumptuous evening. As the whisky and wine flowed the tributes to the gallant and hardworking member became fulsome. 'Whatever happens, we could never have again such a wonderful constituency MP'. 'Hear! Hear!'. 'Not only a politician, but a distinguished scientist and a brave soldier... a wonderful, wonderful MP.' 'Hear! Hear! Hear!'

The guest of honour was genuinely moved and deeply inebriated. His was the final speech. Tears ran down his cheeks. 'My dear, dear friends. I had no idea how much you appreciated my work. It would be treachery if I deserted you now. I will not. I promise I will be your candidate in the General Election.' They all cheered.

In the sober light of day the awful truth dawned. They were stuck with him for another Parliament. He had to be prised out in 1992 with a knighthood and a hint of a place in the Lords in exchange for a promise not to stand again.

In all parties there are sad cases of members who refuse to acknowledge the toll of the years on their bodies and minds. Many have to be pushed because their best friend did not tell them that it was time to jump. For all there is a time to go with decorum and goodwill.

How to Stay Married/ Single

In the sexual stakes Parliament fails to live down to its image. Inevitably, there must be some sexual activity. It is unavoidable where several thousands of sexually active people, separated from their spouses, live jowl by cheek for long periods of the day. No doubt there are furtive encounters in Parliamentary offices when resistance levels are falling and testosterone levels are rising. Some serial seducers of both sexes roam the corridors.

But rampant lechery is still uncommon. Exhaustion is an effective bromide for the great majority of Parliamentarians.

The prime motive for Parliamentary infidelity is the divergence of interests between partners created by Parliamentary work. The good MP must be deeply absorbed in the work. If those interests are not shared by the partner, divisions in the relationship appear and widen dangerously.

More relationships are wrecked by the excessive demands of the Parliamentary workload than by the insistent demands of the loins. Relationships are secure and strong if there is shared dedication to the work of the MP. Making your spouse your secretary is the best way to avoid the disruption and heartache of making your secretary your spouse.

Rumours abound of pressures on single Conservative MPs to marry. After one messy scandal it was alleged by one backbencher that a planeload of lobotomised nuns had landed at Heathrow. They had been trained to say in seven languages 'I will stand by my husband however he humiliates me.' It was claimed that the plan was to line them up in the Commons crypt so that unmarried Tory MPs could select their brides. The Whips would be standing shot gun.

At least one MP in the 1987-92 Parliament bemoaned his loveless marriage which had been urged upon him by puritanically nervous Whips frightened that a scandal would imperil his marginal seat. He related how he had been pressured to 'marry at all costs'. Do women really agree to marriage on these terms? In this case, apparently yes. In the event the couple lost out twice because Labour won the seat in 1992.

The Tory whips are the final repository of homophobia in the House. Labour frontbencher Chris Smith and Tory backbencher Michael Brown 'came out' without any harmful results. In the eighties two other openly gay MPs were involved in a mild public scandal in Germany. One of them unashamedly flaunted his homosexuality and regularly entertained young men in the Commons bars. There was no perceptible effect on their successful Parliamentary careers. They were re-elected with increased majorities. Both are now dead.

Homosexual ex-lobbyist Ian Greer has claimed that there are fifty homosexual MPs still hiding in the closet. As a mathematical probability that is likely. But who cares? The House is tolerant except towards the gay MPs who hypocritically exploit homophobia as a political weapon.

For mysterious reasons, MPs have heightened sexual attractiveness. Many Members are secure on the path of the solitary unmarried state. Prepare for renewed attentions from aspirant sexual or marital partners. Don't be flattered.

How to Behave in a Recess

Recesses are as vital to MPs as the fallow period is to the rotation of crops. It is the time to read, think, write, to shore up knowledge, sharpen interests, recharge the brain cells and restock the mind banks.

The work of the fully staffed office continues. Recesses are the chance to assuage the guilt of not finding enough time to pursue all possible avenues for constituents' complaints. The pace of life slackens agreeably. Schools, charities and factories can be visited. There is time to read the half-understood reports that were published during the session.

But the three month summer recess is far too long. The public are understandably cynical about what they regard as a three month holiday. Most years, Dennis Skinner engineers a vote against it. In 1994 he mustered seventy MPs to vote against. The voters appreciate opposition to months of Parliamentary silence that helps the Government only.

Out of Town

How to Survive Abroad

The annual summer migration follows a ritually ordained pattern. The minion MP becomes metamorphosed into world statesperson. The habitat of grotty flats in Kennington is exchanged for the five star luxury of hotels with exotic names. The car and bus are abandoned for the limousine and club class plane travel – sometimes upgraded to the heaven of 'First Class'.

Shapeless suits are pressed. Plumage is smarter and brighter for the flight to the sun-warmed, fact-filled destinations. It is facts that they are out to find. One Select Committee adviser backed against the wall did confess that the harvest of facts was likely to be thin on one planned odyssey. 'But, not to worry, there are fine nuances of information that can be picked up only by going to the USA.' A 'nuance-finding' trip costing £25,000 for eleven members was a less persuasive proposition. A sliding scale of futility for foreign trips starting from rock bottom would be:

Commercial Jaunts paid for by Greed United plc. Sometimes vaguely wrapped up as study or research tours, their prime function is to stuff large quantities of protein and alcohol into MPs. Ideal for MPs who have decided to prostitute their time to the highest bidder. But it's best to protect the liver and digestion, and quicker and more honest to ask for a straight bribe.

Tyrant's Trips. Dozens of ugly repressive Governments welcome soft-hearted and soft-brained members. The gullible and greedy have been seduced by the heady flattery. Perhaps even a country's President is seeking their advice and help. George Galloway is the supreme 'presidential groupie'. He is on good personal terms with Saddam Hussein, Romania's Illiescu, Benazir Bhutto, and Arafat. Michael Forsyth sneered at George about tripping to Libya. Incredibly Michael chose a county that George had never visited and had to apologise. George has some riveting opening lines, 'The President of Horrorstan told me last week...'.

Military Invasions. MOD and the forces have a colourful brochure of overseas breaks in countries Britain occupies or to odd fragments of the Empire such as Belize. The Falklands is on the list. Great for twitchers and tank spotters prepared to endure the endless refrain from politicians from small countries that they need bombs not butter.

Commonwealth Parliamentary Association Conferences. These are of stupefying banality. Spouses can come along and enjoy the pleasant semi-sober social whirl which occupies three quarters of the time. Chance to rub shoulders with fellow international statespersons and learn from their experiences running the Governments of Isle of Man or Alderney. Recommended for miniaturists because the total budget of some Commonwealth Member countries is less than that of the Commons Catering Committee.

Select Committee Tours. The process for sharing out the available loot is decided by a committee of Select Committee Chairpersons called the Liaison Committee. The process is identical to gypsy horse trading. The agreed tours vary in research content. Some are concentrated studies of serious subjects. Others are shameless jaunts to the far corners of the world to inspect bananas, CD ROMs or techniques of cutting waste in Government spending.

IPU. The Inter Parliamentary Union trips are serious attempts to penetrate alien cultures and erect international bridges. Three quarters of the time is devoted to genuine work. Far better value in time, and avoiding all that tiresome travelling, is to act as a host to IPU delegations visiting Westminster.

Know-How Fund Seminars. Even more worthwhile are the several organisations that use Know-How Fund cash for exchanges with Parliamentarians from Third World countries. The Mother of Parliaments, still has a few things to teach the embryo democracies. No accusations of jaunting will be thrown at members on trips to Tallinn or Ulan Bator in December.

Irish-British Parliamentary Group. This is a uniquely useful body. Under the benign leadership of Peter Temple Morris and Paul Bradbury TD, the two Parliaments have been brought to a closer understanding facilitated by the the lubricants of brogue, blarney and Guinness.

Character Forming Visits. The splendid John Battle once demanded his share of foreign travel from the Whips. Indignantly he protested that he was shouldering Standing Committee burdens for frontbenchers who were constantly abroad. The Whips promised him that 'the very next trip that comes into the office will be yours, John.' It was. He went to the Arctic, training with the SAS – in January.

Martyr Tours. I was invited to visit the Muraroa Atoll in September 1995 to witness the French nuclear tests. The cost to me would have been Aus$5,000. There was no additional charge for the likely nuclear irradiation or the possible experience of being done over by French commandos.

How to Party (Conference)

Party conferences are periods of penance for backbenchers. Listening to a week of speeches from your colleagues and party hopefuls is akin to working a treble shift every day. MPs should not speak to conference unless party bosses insist. The delegates hate their only annual platform being taken over by MPs who have many other platforms. MP speakers should be those in danger of losing their seats in coming elections, or those recruited to grovel to the leadership on some unpopular issue. Doughnutting is permitted.

YOU ARE A BACKBENCHER WITH A LOW MAJORITY

Speaking to large conference audiences requires special techniques. Know your speech by heart. Mark the pauses. Look strong even when the audience does not respond. Check notes only for reassurance, not when speaking. The the speaker's eyes should be focused on a fixed point at the rear of the hall. Never hold notes. A slight nervous tremble in the hand will multiply itself when it reaches the end of the piece of paper into a riveting twitching.

Never correct spoken errors by repetition or apology – unless they are disastrous. Keep the voice strong and pace controlled to the final word of every sentence and the final letter of every word.

Don't slump across the rostrum, or hug it. Stand straight. Use visual gestures sparingly to match the emotion of your words. Craft your original soundbite with care. If successful, the audience for that ten seconds of glory will be the television viewers. Replace the Trafalgar Square Rally voice and style with the quiet intimate tone for the soundbite.

The week is filled with fringe meetings and receptions. They are an inescapable duty and often barely endurable. Many delegates apply the dulling drug of alcohol as a barrier between their inner sensibilities and the exterior hell's pageant.

For the incurable gluttons, free-loaders and winos, receptions can be a joyous spree. There are opportunities for self-expression for the serious politician and the devout hedonist.

Dedicated do-gooders can usefully use their round of events as an exercise in the redistribution of wealth. Eat and drink expensively at receptions organised by fat cats, BNFL, CBI, Swallow Crud Drug Pushers plc, lobbyists, or FOREST. If provoked, ring your aunt in Australia from their receptions. Never eat, but contribute generously to the raffle at the events run by CPAG, Greenpeace, Disability Alliance and Shelter.

The formula for speaking is straightforward. List all sound bites that were applauded in speeches made prior to yours. A glean through previous year's speeches and fringe meetings will produce a good crop. String them together with a little bang start and a big bang finish. All sentences must be simple without sub-clauses. Use words with as few syllables as possible. A quiet voice at the start will force the amplification to be turned up. The crescendo will blow the wax out of the delegates' ears.

Fringe meetings can be informative. Try only those in which the subject is of major interest, where a contribution can be made or a question answered. Avoid the earnest ones in which an unknown is keen to read his thesis on the Russian revolution or give the solution to macro-economic world crisis. Any fringe meeting with jargon in the title will be an endurance test.

Minority British ethnic occasions should be missed by sensitive souls. Scottish Nights are an affront to those of delicate musical, literary or social tastes. Some of the Scots present are determined to reinforce their national stereotype as Rab C. Nesbit. You would be forgiven for mistaking the music for the sounds made by a non-consenting goose being sexually ravaged.

Welsh Nights persist with the mad illusion that all Welsh people can sing. Afficionados find delight in an evening of raffles, beer and a slow desensitising of the brain. It is impassioned sentimentality by the bucketful.

How to Help the Party

A disruptive but essential chore is to work outside of Parliament and the constituency for the party cause. Some attendance at by-elections is mandatory. Most MPs have twinning arrangements with candidates in seats where the party is in a minority. Absence from Westminster delays the work of the office and is inexplicable to Votingham people who want an urgent chat. Acting as a minder for a candidate hideously increases the disruption and confusion.

One MP rashly drank too much in a strange hotel in a by-election and failed to turn up for breakfast. Calls to his room and thumping on the door did not rouse him. He was elderly and his lifestyle made him overdue for a coronary. Alarmed colleagues used the master key to open the door a few inches. It was blocked by the wardrobe that had fallen on the floor. They clambered over the furniture and searched the room.

They could not see him. Sounds of snoring came from the wardrobe. He had got up in the middle of the night, mistook the wardrobe door for the bathroom door, and went inside. No-one knows what happened then but in his efforts to get out the wardrobe fell over. Hours later he was still there happily sleeping like a baby. Two Tory MPs told me this tale about one of their colleagues. The moral of the story in never do foolish things in the company of your gossiping colleagues.

How to Avoid Royalty

Members of the Windsor family are of little or no advantage to an MP. They are a major potential cause of embarrassment and a waste of precious hours of time.

A short guide to royal etiquette:

* Be otherwise engaged when Royalty next visits
    Votingham (and on all future occasions).
* Never accept an honour or a job as Deputy Lieutenant.
* Always rise to toast the Queen. (*sotto voce* you may toast
    'The Queen – and Freddie Mercury. A Great Group!').
* Royal support for good causes can be quoted usefully.
    But never mention their support in the House.
* Royal Garden Parties are best avoided as too wet, too
    hot or too crowded.
* Keep exploring the costs of royalty.

In the twilight days of the monarchy the royals are feverishly thrashing about to find a role. They are no longer the blue-blooded super-beings that stepped out of a fairy tale, nor the ideal of family life after a triple stain of divorces. All that's left is good causes.

Their last fling is to soak up through osmosis credit by association with charities. It is not the royals who are selflessly shoring the charities, it is the charities who are shoring up a dying institution.

Royal occasions are a sinful waste of time and incite emotions of tedium and fury. The sad 'subjects' assemble hours beforehand and wait. Cattle waiting to be slaughtered have a higher status. The sole purpose for the event is to reinforce royalty's delusion of omnipotence by abasing the peasantry before them.

Security is the excuse for the tedium of queues and protocol. The rules are based on the belief that members of public seeing royalty for the first time will try to murder them. Women are expected to curtsy in the presence of an HRH as an acknowledgment that they are inferior mortals to Fergie and Di. To most modern women that's an idiocy too far.

Those who genuinely feel lesser beings to the royals might gain deviant satisfaction from self-abasement on these visits. The MP's only role on their visits is to be an untidy background to their photographs. There are always more useful ways of spending your time.

On two occasions I have had support for campaigns from members of the royal family. Once Princess Di sent me her 'warm good wishes' for a debate I had about improving the lot of young people leaving care. Following 'How to Campaign' advice I had previously enlisted the backing of Lib Dem Diana Maddock and Tory Roger Sims for the issue.

Royal approval multiplied the attention the debate had by several thousand per cent. One news agency misunderstood the message and decided that Di was backing a Labour MP in an attack on the Government. Again there was a wave of attention to a non-existent royal gaffe but also to the plight of youngsters going from full time care to full time neglect.

A similar beneficial boost was given by Di to the anti-landmine campaign. As royalty is being supported by public funds, it is entirely legitimate that their influence should be used to back worthy causes.

In the Chamber

How to Pray

Even at prayer the House is still a writhing posturing political animal. There is a theory that the mood of the country can be gauged by the numbers of Government members at prayer. They increase in proportion to the deepening mood of national anguish.

Presence at prayers guarantees a seat in the Chamber for individual members for the rest of the day. A green 'prayer' card is placed booking the seat for peak attendance later in the day. There are full congregations for budget days and other major occasions.

Opposition MPs rarely use prayer cards, though Dennis Skinner's seat under the gallery is sometimes claimed by the usurping Dennis Canavan or promising awkward squad member Andrew MacKinlay. Dennis Skinner is the only member I have seen who sits during prayers to assert his atheism.

Members of the House stand facing each other for the first prayer then turn to face the back of the chamber for the rest. There are two rival theories about this. It is perhaps a relic of the days when members knelt on their seats to pray. The Serjeant at Arms still does. The other explanation is that prayers once were a shambles. Members made faces at each other in order to provoke laughter. That sounds like the Chamber we know and love.

Once prayers were interrupted by a devout Catholic MP denouncing the hypocrisy of praying while so many people outside were unemployed. There was no known response for an interruption of this kind. The House cannot be suspended if the sitting has not started. But the Member concerned refused to be quiet. Instead he contented himself with making a little history.

Prayers are not witnessed by the public or recorded in *Hansard*. Many Members wait outside the Chamber until prayers are over. Frequently their chattering is heard inside and attendants call them to order.

Under Speaker Weatherill's reign he let it be known among the religious organisations of MPs that he was unhappy that few Labour members attend prayers. Reversing the usual practise, the late Donald Coleman took to dropping in for prayers then usually absented himself from the Chamber for the rest of the day.

There is an unprovable belief that Speakers are more likely to 'call' MPs for questions and speeches if they are in for prayers.

How to Speak

It is not true that Members can sit anywhere in the chamber. A third of places are occupied by the same individuals or party groups.

Not only will a new Member receive hard looks for sitting in territory that belongs to a veteran, there is danger of being sat on. Even where there is no room between two members a veteran will insist on occupying the usual place. The technique is to aim the bottom at the non-existent space between two members, bear down heavily while wiggling the posterior vigorously from side to side. By a phenomenon that puzzles physicists a space appears where there was none before. The bottom of the MP with ancient rights hits the green leather.

The maiden speech is a potentially nervous occasion. The secret of great speaking is not to change the speech but to change the audience. Use the stories and phrases that have gone down well over and over again in Votingham. The words will flow easily and comfortably through familiar waters. Be magnanimous to the previous Member especially if the voters have chosen a new MP by election and dumped a long-serving one. Abandon the venom of the election campaign even if the wounds have not healed. The opponents are now dead meat.

The tradition of non-controversial maiden speeches has been ruptured so frequently that it is no longer obligatory. But a ferocious attack on opponents entitles them to disregard the tradition of hearing a maiden speech in silence.

The first speech is a daunting hurdle. Ignore advice to postpone it for months. Delaying it increases the trepidation. Put a request in to the Speaker immediately after taking the oath. The likelihood is that a slot will be found the following week, in the Queen's Speech debates.

The House will be largely empty, a doughnut of friends assembles and the Chamber's intimacy will quiet jangling nerves. Once that hurdle has been surmounted the Chamber becomes a friendly place.

In theory maiden and all other speeches should not be read. Most are. Notes are permitted and Members frequently read every word. Quotations are not allowed but are used daily through the subterfuge of not announcing that they are quotations. Those who say that they are about 'to quote' are asking for the intervention of the Chair and usually get it.

Backbench debate speeches have plummeted in importance. Whips are often hard pressed to persuade anyone to fill the empty dog hours between 6 p.m. and 9 p.m. The main excitement of peak events of the day is between 2.30 p.m. and 4 p.m.. In the evening hacks and MPs have other things on their minds.

The best hope is that regional media may be interested in a parish pump speech or that *Today/ Yesterday in Parliament* might quote a golden sentence or two. It is rare for either of these programmes to use any but the first or last sentence in the oration.

But they like a bit of colour. John Marek delivered a lengthy, scholarly speech as a frontbench spokesperson on Treasury matters. Alan Beith intervened 'I have been listening to the Honourable Gentleman for twenty-five minutes and I still don't know whether he is for or against this bill.' Marek sighed heavily and replied 'I will come to that later.'

That exchange was the only part of John's splendid, carefully prepared homily that was broadcast in *Yesterday in Parliament*. A lesson to us all.

How to Address

Everyone has done it, at least once. The universal error is to misuse the word 'you'. The occupant of the Chair alone is 'You', everyone else is addressed in the third person. That is the only bit of the archaic verbal rituals that modern MPs should respect. Punishment is swift with howling from opponents and a correction from the Speaker or Chairperson. The other forms of address are flummery against which progressive MPs should be subversive. As a concession to the sensitive all Members can be addressed as 'Honourable'. It is the least accident-fraught address for all.

There is no point in finding out who is 'Right Honourable' and who is 'Honourable'. The tags are always changing and members constantly get it wrong. Why bother? It is positively beneficial to avoid the used of 'learned', as in the 'Honourable and Learned Member for...'. Outrageously the only 'learned' Members are senior barristers. An MP who has won a Nobel Prize for science is 'un-learned'.

'Gallant' is another piece of old fashioned snobbery that should be buried. Its use is confined to a commissioned officer in the Forces. A private who had won a Victoria Cross is not 'gallant'. The sprogs of the aristocracy, the sons of dukes or earls, are entitled to the courtesy title 'the noble Lord, the member for...'. Now it is only used by members out to get a mention in a newspaper diary as 'creep of the week'.

Jeremy Hanley helpfully innovated a new form of address at a committee meeting in February 1997. He forgot the Great Grimsby constituency of Austin Mitchell and referred to him as 'the member with his face on his tie.' Wrong, Jeremy. It was definitely Mick Jagger's face.

But he may have started something. The 'one in the blue pullover' or the 'lady with the pink dress' is much easier to remember that the rest of the antiquated, confusing mumbo-jumbo.

There is no chance of making mistakes when Members refer to 'the last speaker in the debate', 'the Member below the gangway', or 'the Lady opposite'. By a magic process your words will expand in *Hansard* to 'The Right Honourable and Learned Member for Cwmscwt (Mr Llywelyn)'. *Hansard* are the last defenders of an archaic system that reinforces the class-ridden mores of an earlier age.

While there is no list of forbidden epithets that are out of order, objection has been taken to the following: coward, hypocrite, git, blackguard, hooligan, rat, swine, stool-pigeon, traitor blackguard and shit (when used to described a Minister). George Foulkes was forced to withdraw the word when he described Douglas Hogg as an 'arrogant little shit'. During Hogg's recent performances on food safety George has been tempted to request that the word be re-instated as a fair and accurate description of the Minister.

When Tam Dalyell said that the Firth of Forth Bridge was 'encrusted with seagull shit' it was allowed. 'Lickspittle' is not allowed when applied to Members but can be used to describe non-members or strangers. In a ground-breaking event in January 1997 Ian Pearson used the word 'crap' to describe job schemes and was not challenged.

How to Recover from Crash Landings

Inevitably there will be disasters. The key fact disappears from memory in mid-speech. Simple words become unpronounceable or come out backwards. The punchwords will be spoken in the middle of the oral question, leaving a floundering feeble final sentence.

An impassioned plea will be interrupted by the Speaker explaining that the question has already been answered ten minutes earlier. An opportunistic question to the Prime Minister is halted because it is a closed question. Worst of all, there will no words at all. The mind and lips freeze up. An Oral Question may be disastrously untrue and comprehensively flattened by a Minister. There are countless ways to suffer humiliation in Parliament.

Crash landings strike novices and experienced Members. Cultivate a state of constant nervousness. Fear will enforce thorough preparation. The spectre of failure will discourage rash risk taking when unexpected opportunities arise.

Work is the best material to use to bury the memory of embarrassment. It is futile to endlessly repeat the incident in your mind, finding dozens of ways of getting it right — next time. Many politicians waste energy perfecting the speech they made yesterday, not the one that will make tomorrow. Obliterate the memory by refusing to read about it, listen to it on the radio or talk about it. That only deepens the wound. Time will heal and dull the pain. Then laugh at it.

Tony Lloyd now cheerfully recalls what must have been an excruciating experience. His question to Mrs Thatcher was based on an evening paper's claim that Peter Walker had been rebellious in cabinet meeting earlier in the day. Confidently Tony taunted Thatcher on this cabinet split. His confidence was shaken by the Thatcher's cheery smile and the giggles from the Treasury bench. Tony was then pulped by Thatcher's answer. Peter Walker was not only not present at the Cabinet, he was in China.

The House judges everyone by their last performance in the Chamber. Make sure that a stunner is delivered very quickly to smother the nagging memory.

How to Survive the Speaker

Only the foolhardy underestimate Speakers. They have earned great powers through winning the respect of the Chamber. Head-on challenges from backbenchers strike solid rock.

As a very senior backbencher, the late Eric Heffer, insisted on being called to speak. When Speaker Weatherill refused he stood in protest before the mace. Speaker Weatherill surrendered but said that it was 'an abuse of the House'.

It was a rare, possibly unique, occasion. Weatherill's authority was diminished. Many others ruefully recall the wounds of similar encounters. Unforgettable was a blood-curdling telling off delivered on a Friday morning by Speaker Boothroyd to Labour's Ann Clwyd. It was several minutes of detailed accusations and threats. All because Ms Clwyd was guilty of parking her car in the Speaker's Court. But it was early in Betty Boothroyd's Speakership. We all understood who was boss.

Expulsion from the Commons is now almost always contrived. Once it made headlines and could be damaging to individual MPs. Now it is used routinely to make a strong point.

Dale Campbell-Savours is probably the current record expellee. He is convinced that it does no electoral damage and is helpful in highlighting important issues. So frequently has it been used, it has lost its force and is now ignored by the media.

Speaker Boothroyd skilfully sidesteps confrontation. Instead of complaining provocatively that members should wind up because they have spoken too long, she deploys her considerable charm by saying 'I am sure the Honourable Member is about to wind up these interesting remarks'.

Antagonising a Speaker is a kamikaze ploy. Backbenchers can swiftly become invisible, ignored in debates and passed over for opportunist questions. Imposed silences are bitter fare for professional communicators. Only slightly better is being called late in a debate and cramming a lovingly-prepared thirty minute oration into a breathless five minute gabble.

There is now a scientific pecking order of precedence on the Speaker's database. Criteria include seniority, knowledge of subject, frequency of speaking and immaculate behaviour records. Still, as always, most members are convinced that they are treated unfairly.

Prize a good relationship with the Speaker. The rewards include:

* Called early in questions, debates.
* Included on trips abroad.
* Invited to Speaker's dinners.
* Allowed to break minor rules of debate.
* Allowed to make mini-speeches under the guise of
    Points of Order/ Business Questions.
* Given latitude on irrelevant or opportunist questions.
* Generosity on orderliness of Written Questions.
* Expanded time allowed for Oral Questions.

How to Dilute Boredom

Hours of mind-sapping boredom are the inescapable lot of legislators. There is no escape from enduring other backbenchers' speeches while waiting to be called in debates or committees. Erudite, witty and well-informed contributions are rare in the vast dross and dribble of the meandering streams of verbiage. Speakers are called in accordance to their seniority.

The eternal fate of junior backbenchers is to endure hours of emptiness before their names are called. These should by productively filled.

★ *Rework the speech.* Silently voice it to spot weakness and verbal trip wires like difficult pronunciation. (Don't do this while doughnutting in the camera's view. Silent goldfish mouthings will be taken as proof of incipient insanity in Votingham.) Eliminate accident-prone words that knot the tongue: pluralism, statistical, proliferation, similarly, remuneration, mayoralty. Some easily spoken words become unpronounceable when preceded by others.

★ *Familiar expressions* have a habit of coming out upside down. Bill Cash once mentioned 'the prodigal son on the road to Damascus'. Norman Lamont denounced his own party opponents as the 'Flotsam and Bobtail' of politics. John Wilkinson said we must continue to sell arms abroad so that we do not 'cut off our noses to spoil our throats'.

★ *Write* a five minute and a two minute version of the speech. There must be strong opening and closing sentences. Often that is all the time left for last MP in the queue of speeches.

★ *Work.* Long-neglected reports can be read. Write Parliamentary Questions on subjects that suggest themselves by the debate. Collect mail and hand write replies.

★ *Play.* Low spirits and exhaustion will kill the work impulse. To avoid permanent brain abuse from the corrosive boredom try playing. The most deadly speech by other MPs can be entertainingly analysed. Write down:

Grammatical errors.

The most stupid sentence.

The longest/ most platitudinous sentence.

The largest number of repetitions of the same point.

The most self-admiring comment.

Contrast the words spoken with underlying meaning.

★ *Fantasise.* One MP confided to me that much of his empty time in the Chamber agreeably speeds by in dreams of the *Hansard* writers or 'goddesses' as he described them. They perch on high above the MPs in the gallery hanging flatteringly on their every word. When press and public have deserted the Chamber they are loyally ever present to raise drooping spirits.

How to Doughnut

The MP speaking is the hole in the doughnut. The doughnut is the circle of faces, knees and bellies that surround the speaker in the television frame. The doughnut is a living thing, yawning, scratching, dozing, chattering and, just occasionally, listening attentively. Half a dozen MPs make a doughnut. Uniquely Cyril Smith, past member for Rochdale, was a whole doughnut in himself.

An unruly doughnut is fearsome. It fascinates and hypnotises the viewer. One Cabinet Minister had the misfortune of having a backbencher perched above his left shoulder during a critical speech. The backbencher was obsessed with his nose. First he scratched it. Then he blew it noisily with energetic flapping of a handkerchief. Then rubbed it. The performance eclipsed the Minister's words.

Roger Stott suffered a similar fate. He was earnestly addressing the House from the Dispatch Box on the serious matter of Northern Ireland. Emanating from Roger's head a shoe appeared. Then disappeared. Appeared again and bounced up and down rhythmically. It was Tam Dalyell sprawled lengthways in the seat behind. He had his legs crossed performing some energetic footwork. Roger should have saved his breath. No television viewer listened to a word.

The Dispatch Box is the least flattering spot from which to address the House. The doughnut is exposed and the camera angle is cruel especially to bald heads.
The foreshortened bird's eye view makes MPs look like pygmies shouting from the bottom of an untidy green pit.

The prime perch is now the back bench. There the background is handsome oak panelling that never distracts or walks out. Attention is concentrated on the speaker at the most favourable camera angle of eye level.

Elsewhere, dedicated doughnutting can be an asset. A lacklustre speaker can sound like a Cicero with a skilled group of adoring friends. Their attention to the speaker must be constant. Cultivate the absorbed stare of a worshipping angel in an El Greco painting.

Body language should be that of a reverential supplicant. No folded arms, legs crossed to the speaker, perpetually expecting jewels of humour and erudition. The gestures of nodding heads, jaws dropped open aghast, slapping thighs, head in hands in despair are useful when used sparingly and with caution.

Vocal backing from the growled braying of the Dalek-like Parliamentary 'Hear, hear' is basic. Skilled support comes with judiciously intoned 'Ohs!' that can express shock, amazement or disgust. Variation is vital in one word exclamations of 'Disgusting', 'Scandal', 'Exactly', 'Of course', and 'Absolutely'.

The soundbite that is likely to be relayed to the masses is contained in the final words of any speech. However banal or fluffed the last sentence is it must buttressed with loud heartfelt 'Hear, hear'.

Negative doughnutting is a subtler art. Body language and facial expressions should express rejection, contempt and derision. If the speaker turns for support, a shake of the head or eyes imploring the heavens in despair are confidence-sapping. Hyperactive twitching and writhing will destroy the television viewer's concentration on the speaker. During the final sentence of the peroration conspicuously walk out.

How to Nickname

Name-calling is the lowest form of Parliamentary invective. But nicknames are devastating in undermining the confident speaker and destroying the nervous.

The best are brief, true and wounding. They hit their target by highlighting a weakness in the victim's character, appearance or history. Reminders of unfortunate incidents in the past hit the spot. Current popular ones include 'Gorillagram' for David Mellor as the only MP who could earn a living delivering gorillagrams without the aid of monkey suit. Anne Widdecombe had a penchant for wearing all black outfits with little crucifixes dangling from various parts of her anatomy. That earned her the title of 'Doris' (Karloff). Shouts of 'Taxi' and sheep noises inevitably torment Patrick Nicholls and Quentin Davies as reminders of discomfiting incidents from their pasts.

The most startling hair in the Chamber is the blond profusion of Michael Fabricant, which fascinates sketch writers. The Table Office refused to accept a question asking what the Government intended to do to improve the standards of wig-making in Mid Staffs (his constituency). They said it was tabled in the spirit of mockery.

During the Monmouth by-election Jack Cunningham called Tory candidate Roger Evans 'Toad of Toad Hall'. Unfortunately the Welsh hacks were not familiar with Jack's broad northern English accent. They carefully wrote in their note-books 'Turd of Turd Hall'. Luckily the name has not stuck. Roger is remembered for the country suits he wore. They looked like re-cycled grow bags. 'Grow Bag' survives.

During his period as Transport Minister the weighty Robert Key earned the title of the 'Colossus of Roads'; the white pallor of veteran member Dr Alan Glyn suggested the title of 'The Stalking Hearse'.

A spell as Minister of Food left the gargantuan Nicholas Soames nicknamed 'Butter Mountain'. During John Redwood's leadership bid his similarly to Mr Spock from the planet Vulcan damaged him. There had been rumours that the reason that, as Secretary of State, he never spent a night in Wales was because he was beamed up to another planet where he slept hanging upside down from the roof of a cave.

Other current nicknames include 'Martin' (Bormann), 'White Golliwog', 'Action Man', 'Eva Braun', 'The Yorkshire Nipper', 'Steptoe'.

There is a theory that MPs grow to resemble their constituencies in the same way that people grow to look like their pets. A fine example is Henry Bellingham (Norfolk North West) whose profile is remarkably like a turkey. The zombie features of Jacques Arnold are eerily reminiscent of his constituency of Gravesham. Kenneth Baker could represent nowhere but Mole Valley.

Steven Norris is a convincing troll and sits for Epping Forest.

The pixieish Paul Tyler is MP for Cornwall North and Paddy Tipping is everyone's image of Little John. He battles for Sherwood.

Animal nicknames flourished when London Zoo launched a publicity stunt. All MPs were invited to twin fellow MPs with an animal in the zoo's collection. Many of the suggestions were wonderfully wicked. The glittering, sharp-tongued Teresa Gorman was matched to a Jewelled Wasp. Mud-slinger-in-chief of the Tory backbenchers earned David Shaw a twinning with an African Dung Beetle.

On the other side of the political divide Labour's spin doctor Peter Mandelson was judged to have lot in common with a Smooth Snake, and diminutive Welsh MP Ray Powell was linked with a Fat Tailed Scorpion. It was his political role rather than his appearance that earned Dennis Skinner the pairing with a Red Spitting Cobra. Personality compared Anne Widdecombe with a Vulturine Guinea Fowl, David Alton with a Bleeding Heart Tetra and Jacques Arnold with a Malagassy Hissing Cockroach.

Their rare physical attributes produced immediately recognis-able look-alikes for Michael Portillo as a Thick-Lipped Grey Mullet, Hugh Dykes as a Shovel-Nosed Sturgeon and George Gardiner as a Lappet-Faced Vulture. High cheek bones and falling jowls secured for Welsh MEP Glenys Kinnock the nom-ination as a Meerkat and Welsh MP Paul Murphy that of Wart Hog.

How to Insult

Insult is a desperate tactic. The injuries to mega-egos often never heal. Michael Foot said that Aneurin Bevan's career was blighted by long smouldering resentments by fellow MPs that he had insulted.

There is no fury like a woman MP scorned. Out of sight and hearing of the cameras there was a furious row after a Ten Minute Rule Bill debate. Labour's amiable Dennis MacShane wondered what had hit him. Unwisely he said that all the House 'loved' Tory firebrand Teresa Gorman who he then mysteri-ously called a 'chirping gorilla'. How can a gorilla chirp? This drivel infuriated veteran Labour MP Gwyneth Dunwoody, who pinned Dennis to the green leather with a tirade on how not to patronise women MPs. Dennis was left white-faced and shaken.

What was probably a unique walk-out took place in protest to a litany of insults against public figures in Wales delivered by Rod Richards. All Opposition MPs left their seats and walked to the bar of the House. Many public figures were tarred with Richards' indiscriminate brush. Since then Shadow Welsh Secretary Ron Davies has refused to give way to him in speeches because he does not 'respect the rules of courtesy of the House'.

How to Prepare Impromptu Remarks

All MPs can make speeches. The special terror of the Commons at all levels is intervention. It is not enough to read a prepared script or to give a straight from the shoulder rant. An MP must answer 'interventions'. There is no respect for those who refuse to 'give way'.

Increasingly 'interventions' are scripted by the Whips. Lists of single sentence questions are handed out to backbenchers. They are designed to trip up frontbench speakers on big occasions. The most difficult ones to handle are those that seek answers on matters of fact. 'Could he explain what his Government did about earnings disregards in 1964?', 'What was the level of employment when his party was last in office?'

The simplest interventions are the deadliest because they rob the speaker of thinking time. Recently the repeated question of 'What will the Opposition spend on this if they ever get into Government?' wears down speakers weary of their own repeated answer.

The only form of defence is to painstakingly prepare an array of 'impromptu' answers. Many of the interventions can be intelligently anticipated and apposite quips written. Often answers that are slightly off target can be anticipated.

A study of regular attenders on the subject of the debate being discussed will suggest killer retorts against them. They can be irrelevant to the subject of the intervention if they are personal to the questioner. A good riposte will be appreciated by the

House, long after they forgotten what the original question.

On committees it is much easier with a limited number of a dozen MPs. The mines of information are Andrew Roth's *Parliamentary Profiles*, Registers of Interests and Parliamentary League Tables There are some delicious details in everyone's past speeches, electoral history or previous incarnations. If a smart response to an intervention doesn't spring to mind, hit out with an insult. Have a quiver full of lambasting sound darts, ready to throw.

A model Commons performer, George Foulkes and I were locked in animated private conversation during Oral Questions one afternoon. The voice of the Speaker broke through our argument. George started. He tore the Order Paper from my hand to check the number and shouted 'Number six, Madam Speaker'. He had forgotten that he had tabled a question.

The Minister's brief reply allowed no time for George to find out the subject of the question. Powerfully he gave his omnibus supplementary that is good for all occasions. 'That's exactly the sort of answer that I expected to have. It proves again the total incompetence, indifference and lack of compassion of this awful Government. Isn't time for them go? Let's have a Labour Government.'

We all cheered. Mostly for George's recovery from the brink of public humiliation. That supplementary question had been lodged for years in the recesses of his mind ready for that occasion. Government backbenchers similarly caught short would say 'I am most grateful to my honourable friend for that encouraging reply, that proves again.. . (the rest is the reverse of George's question).

How to Be a Hooligan

Rowdyism is a hallowed Commons tradition. Compared with previous centuries the house is seemly and courteous. The cameras have helped. Votingham disapproves if an MP bearing their town's name behaves like an oaf. Misbehaviour is now furtively out of sight of the camera or communal, where numbers obscure identity.

Tony Blair is the target of organised yobbery. The weapons

deployed to destroy his composure are noise, body language and gesture. The ambient noise is often deafening but is diminished by microphones that are distance sensitive and enlarge the dispatch box speech in relation to the background bedlam.

Hundreds of bodies opposite the Dispatch Box wrapped in body language rejection contortions are a formidable confidence sapper. Dismissive synchronised gestures undermine composure. A new ploy is to mirror the gestures of the Labour Leader in a mocking pantomime.

John Major is greeted with mysterious Woody Woodpecker noises. Quality hooligans wait for Major's pauses to dynamite his argument. He often treads into the quicksand of rhetorical questions. His staccato delivery leaves second long gaps in his flow that are filled with shout of 'Wriggling', 'Pathetic' 'Boring', 'Resign'. The hazard of sedentary yelling is pushing the Speaker into fury.

The first rule of professional yobbery is to hit and shut up. Repeated catcalls are dangerous because the Speaker might have homed in on the first shout and if repeated her gaze will be sharply focused on the offender. She is proud of her eagle eye sight. Rod Richards a few days before he was made a Minister by Major shouted 'Liar' when Peter Hain was asking a question. He repeated it a few seconds later and was forced to apologise by the Speaker, twice – first to the House, then to her.

He also broke the second rule. His mouth was not shielded from the Speaker's view by an Order Paper or the bulk of another MP. On a rare lapse when I once unwisely shouted some monosyllabic advice to the Prime Minister I was shielded by the frame of George Foulkes. Betty Boothroyd 'named' the aghast, dumbly protesting George. He was having a rare quiet afternoon. Betty was unrepentant when I confessed my guilt. She had taken George's previous fifty offences into account.

How to Intervene

One of the glories of the British Parliament is the open door backbenchers have to question and humble the mighty. The most obscure backbencher can intervene in party leaders' speeches on almost any occasion. The more obscure the Member the more likely the Speaker is to allow the intervention. All Prime Ministers and Leaders of the Opposition have had speeches wrecked by interveners who have hit the bull's-eye.

Whips from the main parties now routinely distribute model interventions. They are useful but dangerous. Never be the first to use one. Both Major and Blair have pummelled interveners because they have had copies of their opponent's questions that have been left on photocopiers. For original questions the best time is to intervene is early.

The speaker is allowed a few minutes grace. Stand during a natural pause or when the speaker is moving to a new theme. Others will stand a second later in synchronised intervention. The cry 'Will the Prime Minister give way?' must be immediate, loud and authoritative. If rejected, keep standing at intervals especially if a promise has been made of giving way later.

An obvious failure to honour a promise is worth a Point of Order if the mood of the House is sympathetic. The times when all speakers will give way is when they lose their way in their speeches, have a frog in the throat or are distracted. They will welcome the break to recover.

The crippling interventions are those that are apposite to the theme quote a killer fact or ask an unanswerable question. The spirit of many politicians is sapped by embarrassing incidents in their past. John Major is disturbed by any mention of 'O' Levels, John Prescott is unhappy with taunts about his life as a steward. These are cruel but legitimate weapons in the political arsenal.

William Hague once scored over Tony Blair. Having been taunted on something he had said eighteen years before, Hague asked did Blair 'agree with everything he said eighteen years ago, or did he agree with anything he said eighteen years ago?' Tony Blair acknowledged that he had been hit.

How to Legislate

Even though executive power is ballooning in our elective dictatorships, backbenchers still have a legislative role.

Since 1948, six hundred and thirty-six bills have been brought onto the statute book through the work of backbenchers. There are three ways of initiating legislation.

Presentation Bills are introduced behind the chair. The process is swift and simple. Notice can be given to the Public Office as late as the preceding day. All that is required is a long title that outlines the purpose of the bill. It is then printed on the Order Paper and the Member has to be present to hand it to the Clerk of the House when called to do so by the Speaker. Most presentation bills are going nowhere on the legislative conveyor belt. They are for publicity or act as embryo ideas for future bills. Nevertheless one hundred and twenty-five of them are now law.

The fortunate dozen members a year who win high places for Ballot Bills have succeeded on three hundred and fifty-seven occasions. Success or failure is often determined by the choice of bill. Seeking genuine reform is hazardous. Major successes were achieved by Leo Abse who challenged the prejudices of his time on homosexuality and divorce. He was a backbencher by choice, operating from a secure constituency base with a network of cross party contacts. Triumph here depends not on having many friends but having few enemies.

The fate of all Private Bills is in the hands of Government. Reforms can only get through by compromise. Government Whips are always ready to blow them out of the water. Outside bodies are now almost essential in campaigning beyond Parliament to build support and put constituency pressure on MPs.

Small victories are the rewards for bills that have Government support and enjoy a fair wind through the House. Most of Michael Shersby's bills provoked little opposition. He has put a record eight on the statute book. He tells me that it needs 'two years hard work' to succeed. Most of it is persuading Ministers and backbenchers of Government and Opposition to give the bill a fair wind.

The Lords have chalked up ninety-five bills and even the disregarded Ten Minute Rule Bills have had fifty-nine successes. Diligent and intelligent planning and luck can secure committee time for Ten Minute Rule Bills.

But Private Bills are a gargantuan thief of time. Instant success is rare. Apparent failure is reversed by later bills by other members or rewarded in heaven.

How to Use Ten Minutes

Moving or opposing Ten Minute Bills are prime weapons in the backbencher's armoury. At best they deliver a captive audience of the House and the live television audience for a topic of the Member's choice.

To secure a bill slot the MP must be first in the queue outside the Public Bill Office at 10 a.m. on the specified mornings. Until recently an all night wait was an essential penance to win first place. Now matters are often agreed with civilised arrangements between the Whips. It may not last. Sensible dealings are alien to our Parliamentary traditions.

A minor crisis developed in December 1996 when I turned up at 4 a.m. and found two sleeping bodies. There were four slots on offer that day to be allocated at 10 a.m. Daylight revealed that in addition to two sleeping Labour Members, Tories Elizabeth Peacock and Andrew Rowe had bagged places the night before. Then, it was presumed, they went off to sleep at home. Peacock had left a teddy bear behind garlanded with the message 'I am Elizabeth Peacock's research assistant queuing for a Bill for LIFE.'

Elizabeth Peacock argued that it was not reasonable for her to have spend the night with three bearded Labour MPs in order to get a bill. John Heppell and Paddy Tipping were a little hurt. I magnanimously declined to press my claim and Peacock had her bill. The Whips gave me the next slot, but the system is long overdue for reform.

When a place is won at the head of the queue, the procedure is simple. All that is needed is to provide the clerk with a long title of the bill stating its purpose. Pack information into the title to intrigue and excite the hacks. The form is that the Member 'begs leave to introduce a bill to abolish the monarchy/ to introduce daylight saving/ to Reform the Electoral law'. Add the coda 'and for connected purposes' to include all the extra ideas that will crop up in the fortnight's wait before the bill is presented to the House.

Heaven is starting the speech precisely at 3.30 p.m. with a full house present, inherited from Prime Minister's Question Time and perhaps waiting to hear a vital debate that follows. Hell is having the slot delayed by a sensational Government statement on a juicy scandal, followed by a hour of questions. The hacks have their story for the day. They and the MPs will have deserted the Chamber by the time for Ten Minute Bills.

Ten minutes is an ocean of time for those skilled in squashing arguments into three brief sentences. The perfect ingredients for the speech are a riveting start, a punchy finish, two or three good jokes and persuasive middle that makes a positive case and demolishes any reply from your opponents. Time the speech for eight minutes to allow for rhetorical flourishes.

It is fatal to try to cram too much in and garble the denouement. Often a division is useful but is best organised with (unofficial) co-operation with the Whips. On the day the Public Bill Office will prepare for the Member a Dummy Bill and a copy of the choreography. It is a surprise to read the details of the rigmarole for marching from the Bar of the House to the table. 'Five steps and bow, another five steps and bow.' Quaintly, it concludes, 'Then hand your Dummy to the Clerk.'

Opposing someone else's Ten Minute Bill is tricky. Intelligent research on the mover's part will almost always explain the line of argument that will be used. Give notice to the Speaker as early as possible of the intention to oppose. There may be a queue. Listen intently to the speech. The House always appreciates a good debating speech that could not have been rehearsed.

It is essential to shout 'No' when the Speaker calls for those for and against even if a vote is not wanted. Explain to the Speaker what is happening and shout in a whisper. A futile or an abortive vote will drag hundreds of Members away from their desks, will anger friends, delight enemies and may shift votes against the bill. An unwanted vote can steal the time available for later important debates.

Vast quantities of luck, arm-twisting and guile can get Ten Minute Rule Bills into committee and onto the statute book. It happens rarely, but times may be changing.

How to Petition

Hardly anyone understands petitions. Their history is arcane and extraordinary. Petitions to Parliament have suffered centuries of hostility. One presented by the Mayor of Salisbury in 1640 was ordered to be burnt. Not much has changed since.

In the last century ten thousand a year arrived. Twenty years ago the number had slumped to about forty a session. Recently they have picked up twenty-fold. Single issues, particularly on disability or animal welfare, have excited new epidemics of petitioning.

Constituents should be warned of the limits of the value of this approach in mobilising opinion and creating publicity. They should also be informed of the obligatory archaic preamble that the House requires and the need to hand write the first page. Every petition must begin 'To the Honourable the Commons of the United Kingdom of Great Britain and Northern Ireland in Parliament Assembled' and end 'and your petitioners, as in duty bound, will ever pray, &c'.

MPs only can present petitions, either by dropping them in the green bag behind the Speaker's Chair while the House is in session or verbally present them on specific occasions. Prior to the second reading of the Alton Bill and at other times petitions have been used as a time-wasting ploy to delay discussion.

The tradition of minimal interest inside the House continues in spite of the recent revival of extra-Parliamentary enthusiasm. There is an Act still in force saying that no petition can be presented by more than ten persons. It is quaintly called the Act Against Tumultuous Petitioning, passed in 1661, and could still be invoked to block any petition that was likely to be taken seriously.

The only historic relic still operating in their favour is that uniquely petitions can be sent to the House post free. Some constituents still believe that letters to MPs are post free, as all Members occasionally discover to their cost.

How to Win Prizes

There is little tangible evidence for backbenchers to prove that they are doing a good job.

No one admits to being interested, of course. But in the small hours of morning many MPs secretly live out the fantasy as being acclaimed as the 'Parliamentarian' or 'Backbencher' of the year. They are a balm for sorrows of the wounded ego, a bolstering comforter for underloved toilers in the Parliamentary vineyard. The chances of success are minute.

Trying to win disqualifies. The awards are provided by the right wing *Spectator* magazine with the help of a Scottish whisky company. The choice is made by ten political writers from the serious papers.

Dave Nellist candidly acknowledged when he was named Backbencher of the Year that the prize was intended to embarrass the Labour Party. The same party later expelled him for his connections with Militant Tendency. He was certainly a lively backbencher but there were a dozen others equally deserving of the award. Roger Berry and Richard Shepherd won the backbencher awards for brilliant work on Private Bills. John Redwood and James Callaghan got their awards as proof that backbenchers could make it after spells on the front line.

Tam Dalyell had a unique mention in 1984 as 'Troublemaker of the Year'. The most prophetic choice occurred in 1991 when the 'Member to Watch' was David Mellor. The awards are given at a swish lunch at the Savoy. A waspish citation should be answered by a few self-deprecatory jokes.

The steaming climate of jealousy of the Palace of Westminster is hostile to prize winners. Parliamentarians/ Backbenchers of the Year can expect a chilling of friendship. It is better to secure the Parliamentary Campaign for Freedom of Information award, the Parliamentary Friend of Small Businesses prize or the Greenest MP gong. They agreeably boost stature in Votingham but are not prestigious enough to incite envy.

Even less damaging are the burgeoning awards for tiny specialist triumphs. They may well be prizes for Parliamentary Friend of Cement, Promoter of Butterfly Conservation or even the Most Abject Lickspittle of the Lord Lieutenants. They harmlessly make Members big fishes in a few tiny ponds.

The flood of information from the House of Commons databases provides insight into Parliamentary activities. League tables are compiled of the numbers of divisions attended, speeches made and questions asked. Attendance registers at committees exist that identify the habitual truant. The measure is quantity not quality. Sadly no one can assess the value of the worth of the contributions in the league tables. They are a crude guide to activity. It is a sore embarrassment to the inactive members who record *nul point* for Parliamentary work.

Paul Murphy was feeling very hard done by late one Thursday night. He was one of the few members left in a deserted House. His day had been spent slaving on a Housing Bill long after most MPs had gone home. He was told in a telephone message that HTV had produced a league table of Welsh MPs, analysing who was doing the most work. The sad news was that he was almost bottom as the least hard working MP. The worst news was that the two Members below him in the table were both dead.

Increasing publicity for these league tables sometimes has a galvanising effect. A shame list of non-speakers in one session prompted most of them to break their silence within the following fortnight.

Advanced Steps

How to Squirrel

Odd sums of money arrive in the post. Cheques from the media interviews, for writing or from market research companies are not really earned. They are usually paid for doing the job for which MPs are already paid.

If they lie heavily on the conscience, they can be diverted into a fund for excess income. Set up a proper charitable trust with defined aims and trustees, into which the full sums can be deposited. A simpler course is to pay tax on the cash, then deposit it in a separate charitable account with independent signatories.

Either way the sums quickly accumulate into substantial amounts for worthwhile giving. They avoid dependence on outside money and ensure that work priorities are not distorted by financial temptations. Always insist that any charitable giving is anonymous. It absolves the giver of the insulting charge of trying to buy votes and it reduces the calls on the fund from unworthy causes.

How to Survive Unpopular Causes

The two biggest avalanches of mail that overwhelmed the Commons' efficient Post Office in the past decade sprang from the Alton Bill on abortion and the implementation of the Poll Tax.

Many angry constituents' letters have a sting in the tail threatening not to vote for the incumbent MP in the General Election. In most cases this is a vacuous ploy. There are few issues that determine voting habits in General Elections. Mostly they are determined by how the national policies of parties serve the material self interest of voters. On issues of conscience a firm position should be taken as soon as possible. Expressing uncertainty invites furious lobbying from all sides.

Factions are quick to identify those with strong opinions that cannot be moved. They concentrate on the waverers. I received letters, petitions and calls from ten per cent of my constituents on the Alton Bill because I had expressed genuine doubt. On hanging I had less than a dozen letters because I had long said that I would never vote for a restoration of capital punishment. Voters soon recognise an immovable object.

British contemporary politics has slid into the same pit of political cowardice as the USA. There legislators can use their vast allowances to measure voter opinion on all issues. Their votes can always be trimmed to the current prejudice and bigotry of the masses. No doubt, this is a great way to secure an election majority and swell the incumbency factor. But this is not the way for a politicians to operate unless their highest ambition is to be an automaton. A computer could vote slavishly in line with opinion poll results.

Some MPs are mesmerised by the ebb and flow of their majorities. That is the measure of their self-worth. A healthier view is that a bloated majority could prove that the Member is not challenging the baser views of the local constituents.

A progressive MP should charge the barricades of ignorance and bigotry. No worthwhile reform has ever been achieved by obeying the lowest common denominator of public opinion. There will be loss of votes for any current MP backing euthanasia, legalising illegal drugs, modernising royalty, cutting unnecessary NHS operations and drug prescribing, or arguing for humane treatment for prisoners, sites for gypsies, and immigrants' rights.

Supporting any of these subjects will cause eruptions of fire and brimstone from local press, party and voters. With a majority of 1,000 such a course would be perilous. With a comfortable majority it is a positive duty to lead on issues regardless of their popularity.

It is electorally hazardous to be identified with a single unpopular cause. Causes with popular support and constituency issues must be laced into the cocktail of work to create an acceptable brew for the constituents.

Voters loathe hero-worshipping members. They much prefer to say, 'My MP is round the twist on some issues but otherwise a great constituency MP'. Sometimes there's a modest pride in having a highly individualistic character of a MP. Minor eccentricity and notoriety are generously tolerated and preferred to obscurity.

How Not to be Spun

Spin doctors strive to control the Parliamentary web. Employed by the party leaders, their gossamer is used to clog the brains and bandage the mouths of backbenchers. Their 'plot' is to stun backbenchers into a state of continuing manic exaltation of the leader and all his works.

Nothing must be allowed that will slow or divert the majestic progress of the 'plot' of securing General Election victory. The next one and the one after. Their concentration is needle point focused but its span is that of a retarded earthworm. Nirvana to them is a happy headline in the tabloids tomorrow. The day after tomorrow and the rest of the future is invisible, far over their time horizon.

They can help. Their inventive minds produce venomous inspired quips for the sluggish brained backbenchers short of a retort at Prime Minister's Questions. Slothful reporters are supplied with the glowing heaps of words that build and promote the plot of the day.

In the week of the Littleborough and Saddleworth by-election I felt the hot breath of their wrath. For months I had tried to get a debate on legalising the use of cannabis for medicinal reasons. My chance came dangerously close to the date of the by-election for the spin doctors' comfort. Their strategy was to paint the Lib Dem candidate as a drug pushing libertine and canonised the Labour man as an immaculate hermit.

The Lib Dem candidate had advocated a Royal Commission on illegal drug use. Panic broke out when my debate was noticed. I was approached by friendly Whips, a creepy spin doctor and an aggressive backbencher. Their judgement had been twisted into a belief that I was about to give ammunition to the Lib Dems. The plight of many thousands of sick people unfairly deprived of a unique medicine was dismissed by all except Chief Whip Derek Foster. He understood the need for a change in the law because of a constituency victim.

The debate was not widely reported. The voters decided that the Lib Dems had been caught in possession of an intelligent argument and elected its candidate. Labour was rejected on the grounds of implausible sanctity.

The umbilical link between spinners and hacks guarantees that their version of events is reported first. Sometimes to their detriment. On occasions when I have incurred their wrath, their negative briefings have been provocative and damaging to their cause.

At a private meeting of the Parliamentary Labour Party I raged in direct simple language at a piece of party folly. An hour after the meeting, Ceefax carried the spin doctor placed news that I had expressed 'unease'. That word is rarely in my vocabulary, especially that day when emotions were soaring.

The tactic, I believe, was to dilute the true nitric adjectival tirade that they expected me to leak to the hacks. It was counterproductive and gave publicity to an attack that would otherwise have remained private.

Now it is unwise to treat the meetings of the Parliamentary Labour Party or the 1922 Committee as private. Leaking from both has become a flood.

How to Avoid Murder

The MP most likely to be murdered by colleagues is the Select Committee time glutton. Those waiting to pack their allotted time with concentrated interrogation of witnesses smoulder at aimless babbling.

One Select Committee member sharpened his act after being told that his 'bouncing questions' were legendary. Beginning 'Can I bounce this off you,' he spouted a spiral of verbal ectoplasm that wreathed the committee with wayward, futile words, going on ...hypnotically... eternally. Not once did he see the homicidal yearning in the eyes of his colleagues for silence, a full-stop or a question mark.

Also at risk are the pitiable Friday morning debates groupies. The thinly attended Chamber allows the junior, the unloved and unnoticed Members to burble and bore. Chances of publicity and a spot on *Today in Parliament* are increased as there are poorer pickings from the dross. Government Whips nurture the Friday groupies to block and obstruct bills from opponents. The ammunition is filibuster briefings designed to give *ersatz* leaden authority to speakers on the topics of the day.

Time is the executioner of Friday bills. The bores congeal, forming a solid blob to jam the hours from 9.30 to the 2.30 limit when bills are talked out and decapitated. The authors of other bills in the queue fantasise a similar fate for the filibusterers.

The doyen of backbenchers Leo Abse gave me a valuable piece of advice thirty years ago. 'Never speak for longer than three minutes when you are speaking in the open air'. I have always followed it. Even on a warm day with a sitting audience, three minutes is enough because there are many outdoor distractions. An audience standing in the cold, desperate for a rest or a loo will rapidly lose patience.

I DECLARE THIS SPEECH OVER !

In Newport in December 1995 Clare Short spoke for less than a minute and won the eternal love of the audience. Another speaker did not. 'Stop him or there will be a riot,' a friend whispered. It was the opening of Newport's Transporter Bridge and an inexperienced speaker was going on and on.

and someone else called Fred made the handrails, well some of them anyway, with a bit of help from Joe. Or was it Bill?...

He was the third speaker. It was the coldest night in Newport since the Ice Age.

I'd never been down to Newport before, but the other chap Harry, I think had, but I am not sure. Anyway...

A shivering desperate voice in the crowd yelled 'Get on with it'.

He was wildly applauded. The Speaker misunderstood it as appreciation for his lecture

> Thank you, very much. Where I work there is a steel works and a river just like Newport's and a little further on...

The face of Clare Short and those of the rest of the platform party were contorted, frozen in arctic pain.

> And there are sixteen cables in all. Each one of them is made up of a hundred and twenty-seven strands of round wire wrapped together in....

The thoughts of the crowd were elsewhere. How much cable would be needed to garrotte someone? Which bits of the bridge would make the best gibbet?

After an eternity something made him stop. Maybe he heard sobbing from the crowd. Perhaps the penny did drop. A lesson to all open air public speakers, it is time to shut up when your tormented audience is planning to lynch you.

In the bad old days of overcrowded offices, I shared a room with seven MPs plus assorted researchers. Order and tidiness were impossible. Desks disappeared under a tip of papers. To compensate a sign was fixed on the door saying 'A tidy desk is proof of a diseased mind.' We learned to survive in, and to love our squalor – except Paul Murphy. There was never a scrap of paper on his polished desk. Perpetually, it gleamed mockingly at us. His desk was polished and paperless. A frequently contemplated remedy by the other six of us was homicide.

Others who incite similar emotions are those who trample over other MPs' constituencies without prior notice, or muscle in on issues that others have proprietorial rights. The Commons is a village of peculiar people doing a peculiar job. Beware.

How to Persuade Government

A Government is an vast organism internetted and muscled by bonds of self-interest and self-defence. Insensitive and inert, its reaction to new ideas can be precisely predicted.

Insider and well-connected Peter Bottomley let me into the secret five steps to success. Usually there are divided by periods of about six months.

> *Send the idea to the Government.*
> Forever afterwards they will deny ever receiving it.
> *Send it again.*
> They will confess they've seen but they have lost it.
> *Send it again.*
> The third time they will simply say 'No.'
> *Send it again.*
> They say the idea won't work and provide irrational reasons why not.
> *Send it again.*
> Finally they will introduce the scheme and announce that it is their own idea.

Records of the first move in any campaign should be treasured. I prize a cutting of an article I wrote for the July 1974 edition of the RoSPA magazine *Care on the Road.* I had the temerity to argue that lives would be saved if speed humps could placed on public roads. The RAC denounced the idea as 'crazy', RoSPA ridiculed the idea saying it would cause more accidents than it would avoid. The Government followed the first step above and subsequently the other four. Traffic calming has since saved hundreds of lives.

How to Open Government

All Governments are secretive. One element of the denial of information policy in the eighties was to end the printing in *Hansard* of Parliamentary answers from 'next step agencies'. This was a serious loss because almost all the civil service is run by the agencies. It was a special problem for MPs and outside bodies who rely on *Hansard* for news.

Confusingly the questions were printed in Hansard and whetted the appetites. As a frontbencher, photocopying answers to outside bodies grew to be a major office activity. With the help of a grant from the Rowntree Trust and the great work of researcher Tony Lynes, I published a monthly selection of answers called *Open Lines*. Copies were sent to all MPs and many outside organisations.

In the meantime I campaigned with questions for the Government to change policy. After two years they nationalised my private enterprise venture, and answers and letters from agencies' chief executives now appear in *Hansard*.

The daily grind of questions is essential to prevent future Governments slamming shut the door of secrecy.

How to Blaze a Trail

The most widespread talent among MPs is fluency in saying the obvious. Students of Friday debates discover countless repetitions of what is accepted wisdom. It is usually a re-statement of shared prejudice founded on ignorance. A Law and Order speech runs, 'Crime is bad, I want to stop it. More punishment please.'

After a well publicised accident the same theme is repeated by dozens, 'I am sorry and sympathetic. We must stop an identical accident happening again.' An illegal drugs one goes 'Drugs deaths are increasing, the best policy is tough punishment, we must be tougher.'

Only rarely during these orgies of mass-deception do small voices try to ask challenging rational questions. Do longer prison sentences reduce crime? Why debate ten deaths in a rail accident and ignore ten deaths a day on the roads? If drug prohibition is working why do drug use and deaths increase every year? It is not working; so don't fix it?

The only debate I witnessed in which opinions were changed in the House was one on illegal drug use. An amendment powerfully argued by Tony Banks and Diane Abbott urged a new policy to end the prohibition of soft drugs. Two North of England MPs and one from London said that the speeches changed their minds. They had never heard the arguments before.

There are many trails that can be blazed through the Westminster forests of errors and half-truths. The vast powers

145

that Parliament has of inquiry, innovation and law-making are often used as crude blunt instruments. There is great talent and experience among members especially in the fields of the law, industry, trade unions and the arts. Knowledge of science is lamentable, and techniques of scientific thinking are embryonic.

There are scientific institutions in Westminster. The most accessible and useful for Members is the Parliamentary Office of Science and Technology (P.O.S.T.). The magazine *New Scientist* is a treasure house of information for politicians, anticipating new trends as it does.

Regularly Parliament congratulates itself on buying technological jobs from what were recently Third World countries. Rarely do we ask why we have neglected the successes of our own inventive genius for scientific innovation.

Major reforms will be initiated by those who work to put right our neglect of science and who challenge the disrespect for objective reasoning. It is certain that one of the reforms of the next decade will be in reducing harm caused by legal, illegal and medicinal drugs. The case will not be argued by the majority gluttons or those climbing the greasy pole. It will come from backbenchers — especially those who are backbenchers by choice.

How to Walk on Water

Regular excessive demands are made on the understanding and knowledge of MPs.

All have to learn to walk on water. Ignorance is no bar to the daily chore of pontificating on complex matters. The act has been described as 'treading on a sea of bullshit'. The danger of sinking is always imminent.

The public rightly question how mere mortals can be expert on everything, today preaching on nano-technology and income support and tomorrow on BSE and Seamus Heaney. That is the duty of the artisan backbencher. Oral Questions on unknown topics are easy. Front bench teams will provide the three necessary sentences. The Library will turn up the latest editorials and feature articles.

Speeches are daunting. There is the possibility of interventions which will puncture aplomb and expose gaping ignorance. On Standing Committee, opposition backbenchers are frequently supplied with gobbledygook notes by specialist 'advisers'. Reading them convincingly is an acquired technique. Sometimes half-way through a speech, understanding dawns. The speaker begins to get an inkling on what he is talking about.

On one social security bill an amendment was selected for debate that puzzled the frontbenchers. An adviser from a voluntary body had asked for it to be tabled. He was not in the committee and could not be contacted. No committee member could remember its purpose or understand it.

Sensibly, we panicked and withdrew the amendment.

How to Climb the Greasy Pole

An oddly democratic ritual still largely determines the place in the Labour Shadow Cabinet. Liberals are press ganged into similar offices that are perpetually in shadow. In the Conservative Party, God and the Whips whisper the names of the chosen into the party leader's ear.

Voting fodder Labour MPs brace themselves in the autumn for the annual seduction offensive. Colleagues who usually pass by with a curt nod, develop a keen interest in the welfare of the spouse, the kids, the bad foot.

Aspiring Shadow Cabinet members will insist that it is always their round for the tea and carrot cake. Congratulatory notes arrive: 'Your speech on Wednesday was the best thing heard in the House since the time of Gladstone'; 'Would you mind if I copy your brilliantly funny question yesterday for my constituency newsletter?'; 'Will you send me a copy of the speech you made at conference? Everyone is talking about it.'

The flattery is based on the well founded assumption that there are no limit to the vanity of MPs. For many this approach has long been successful. Edward Pearce once commented that the sycophantic approach on one MP was the most impressive display of begging since the mendicant friars of the middle ages roamed the country selling indulgences.

The killer line for one habitually successful candidate was 'I know I won't win this year, because of the quality of the competition. But you will think about voting for me? You won't see me humiliated, will you?'

Sometimes candidates overdo the outside publicity under the strain. Jack Straw once demonised squeegee windscreen washers as akin to muggers in his now famous 'Kick a Beggar for Socialism' speech. Mo Mowlam puzzled the nation when she suggested building a new palace for the royal family. Most people thought this was a bit unnecessary. They have seven palaces already.

Negative campaigning is a new and developing feature among the papers. A 'hit list' of the unworthy Shadow Cabinet candidates appear, and is reproduced in dozens of feature articles. It can be counter-productive and is never as destructive as the traditional malicious whispering campaigns. Life will be blown into old gossip of candidates' frailties and disloyalties. Poisonous anecdotes will be unearthed, malevolently revitalised and broadcast widely.

A new element is the women's assisted places scheme whereby a quota of women candidates must be elected. This prompted one woman MP to suggest that candidates for the Shadow Cabinet should be accepted only after a full medical and psychological examination. Others tried to discredit the system by backing a list of 'noddy' candidates who normally would have had no chance. One of them came close to being elected.

How to Succeed

'When all else fails, lower your standards', was the message on a badge worn by a barmaid in a pub in Marshfield in Newport. The secret of success and happiness in politics is adjusting ambitions to abilities and realistic prospects. For those who get it right straightaway, no lacerating adjustments of standards is necessary.

The belief that all political careers end in failure is based on the myth that all MPs hope to become Prime Minister. They do not. Happiness is keeping as small a space as possible between hope and achievement. Paradise is when they coincide. Here is a scientifically calculated guide to the odds of achieving ambition. Factors have to be applied to the calculation depending on party, age or susceptibility to the seven deadly sins.

Current prospects: odds

Prime Minister: 1000-1
Speaker: 900-1
Secretary of State: 50-1
Chair of Select Committee: 60-1
Junior Minister: 20-1
Disgraced sleazeball: 40-1
Knighted: 4-7(Con) 250-1 (Lab)
A Whip: 7-1
Good constituency MP 8-1

How to be Honoured

The Welsh writer Ellis Wynne in his 'Visions of the Sleeping Bard' described Hell. A uniquely devilish punishment was used against those who in life had titles that puffed them up above the egalitarian herd. They were to suffer each other's pompous company, in hideous fashion, for eternity.

The invisible lure of a knighthood is a potent force in Parliament. Only two Labour MPs have been so honoured in recent years. It is puzzling because the party is opposed to honours. Rumours suggest that the nominations came from the Conservatives. About twelve years of attendance now entitles a Tory to one. The process is accelerated for dumb loyalty in the Whips Office and slowed for any signs of independent thought or action.

The late Robert Adley harangued me for withdrawing the word 'lickspittle' at the request of the Speaker. She allowed me to substitute 'mediocre, talentless and obedient' as a description of MPs who receive knighthoods. Adley never became Sir Robert. He was a great expert on railways, a long serving member but no 'lickspittle'. In respect of all the worthy un-knighted ones, no titles are recorded in this book.

As Labour Members of great distinction and service to the House refuse them, honours are tarnished. They are seen as the rewards for plodders for services to desks or international travel. To the low flyers and the miniaturists they give some consolation and a little distinction especially when they travel abroad. Foreigners still have lingering respect for titles.

A useful subversive ploy is to address all the knights as 'Mister' or all the non-knights as 'Sir'. It creates nervousness. Describing 'Hons' as 'Right Hons' and vice versa distresses those who prize honours. They cannot correct the speaker without revealing their pomposity.

Some new knights are gracious enough to be embarrassed. 'I had to take it, y'know. It's my wife. She's really keen to be Lady Cringe.'

Why knighthoods? Knighthoods are bestowed

* As a badge of mediocrity for undistinguished long service.
* To malcontent political opponents to annoy their leaders.
* To reinforce subservience to royalty.
* To silence aspiring rebels.
* To coax the clapped-out to retire.
* To punish independent MPs by exclusion.
* To reward partial senior civil servants who are 'one of us'.
* Because everyone 'likes his wife'.

How to Use Privilege

Privilege is precious and must be used only with caution.

MPs are protected only for their words in the Chamber or in Committee session. Before a press conference in a House Committee room members of the Transport Select Committee were surprised by a warning that we were not protected by privilege. We had some hard things to say about the dilatory introduction of safety measures on British roll on roll off ferries – or as we learned to call them 'roll on roll over' ferries.

Privilege is a useful 'when everything else fails' threat to name commercial bodies that have badly served constituents. The threat I have used many times but only twice have I carried out. The effect each time was galvanising. The first was against a man who planned to open a power station in my constituency. He had a colourful past which did not inspire confidence that the station would be well run. It was a serious polluter when operated by the C.E.G.B. I named him in an adjournment debate. The plan was dropped and the man left the country.

The other person had harassed two of my elderly constituents rendering uninhabitable the flat that had been their home for twenty-two years. His plan was to open a children's play centre in my constituency. He had many previous business ventures. Four of them had failed after their premises had burnt down. In EDMs I said that he was not the ideal person to run a children's centre. He left the town and the project collapsed.

In both cases I had voluminous evidence and I warned the two people that I intended to name them. Both refused to co-operate and drop their schemes. Although newspapers had a great deal of evidence they were reluctant to use it until I had published it under privilege.

In the first case I had a great body of evidence delivered anonymously to me, I believe from a civil servant. On the second the Welsh Language television programme *Taro Naw* and the *South Wales Argus* collected the evidence and courageously published much of it.

How to Switch Off

The Commons has some little known oases of relaxation. There is a Gym and a Chess Room. Many groups meet to discuss hobbies and interests. There are thriving photographic and painting societies in the House that run annual exhibitions of Members' work. Once a week there are yoga classes. Somewhere in the bowels of the building is a hotly controversial shooting gallery which most Members want to close down and replace with a crèche.

The Gym supplies personal massages. There is even a mobile massage service to Members' offices They are called 'Workplace Energising and Re-vitalising Massages'. The cost is £5 for ten minutes. Sadly the scope for misunderstanding from spouses limits the number of customers.

Multi-channel televisions in most Members' office supply live feeds from the chambers and the main terrestrial and satellite channels. Sky Sports is hugely popular. Annoyingly the service dies if the House adjourns early and the screen goes blank, often in the middle of *Newsnight*. Some sets can be brought back to life by switching them off and on.

The best spot for top quality relaxing is the Terrace in summer. It's a consolation for the most abject moment of political inadequacy in my life. During the the 1992 campaign I shared an election forum with a yogic flyer from the Natural Law Party. He promised the voters 'an end to war, reducing the incidence of all diseases by half and a world that will be suffused with bubbling bliss.' All I had to offer was the minimum wage. There have been times on the Terrace in late summer evenings, sitting watching the drama of the moving river, warmed with a drink and the company of good friends that I have had moments when I felt the bliss bubbling up.

How to Know the Village Folk

Parliament is a village, a lively living community of several thousand people. In addition to members there are secretaries, researchers, police, cleaners, waiters, contractors, a doctor and a hairdresser. Within the confines of the Palace they live, socialise, eat, sometimes even sleep, make love and occasionally die.

Commons staff are a daily link with reality. Performing unpretentious jobs they can be an anchor to reality. Their company and views are worth cultivating. Some are celebrated as Commons' characters.

The most reliable source of information of the dates of recesses or elections is Abdul the lift attendant. He operates and supplies his forecasts from the lift in the corner of the Star Chamber Court.

While many faces come and go in the Members' Tea Room, Jean is the lone survivor. Her public and unashamed crush on Hugh Dykes has aroused comments in the papers. Jean is resigned to the fact that her love must forever remain unrequited. Her unchanging duties are clearing the tables and doing the washing-up. This brings her into frequent contact with Members.

She is always polite and chatty. Her greetings divide the sheep from the goats. Those who have made in it the popularity stakes are welcomed with a 'Good morning, Mr Prescott' or 'Good afternoon, Ms Clwyd'. For ten years I have greeted her with a hopeful 'Good morning, Jean'. Alas her answer consigns me to that anonymous mass of invisible MPs, 'Good morning, dear,' she replies. Will I ever make it?

Everyone has views on Stephen Silverne, the Commons hairdresser. His twenty-seven years in the House give him authority as one of the village's longest serving inhabitants. A haircut is an educational experience. His knowledge of the Jewish community in the East End and the Israeli-Arab conflict is the stuff of legends. Totally unfounded and mischievous rumours claim that he is employed as a Mossad agent.

His styles of cutting hair owe more to the Second World War period than to the era of Oasis. Long may he continue to provide an efficient, accessible service for emergency haircuts. The prices are wonderful value for central London There is no charge for the always stimulating running commentary.

A unique breed of police guard the Palace. There are an unrelated species to the police on *The Bill* or *Hill Street Blues*. Once they planned to bring law and order to the unruly streets of Brixton and Tiger Bay. Perhaps they dreamed of quelling riots or dealing with the hard characters. But then they changed. One day their companions noticed they were different. Perhaps they developed a passion for preserving the marsh fritillaries, making dolls out of raffia or even discussing the subtleties of Plato.

Dealing with criminals no longer held their interest. They were consigned to the police nirvana of Parliamentary duties. Even those who have had bad previous experience of the Metropolitan Police acclaim the Commons Police as kind, considerate and courteous. All MPs say to other MPs 'Aren't our police marvellous?'

Final Steps

How to be Ennobled

The House of Lords is the ideal rest home for the semi-clapped out. The comfort and pampering is enjoyed plus the power to influence policy. Not missed is the nagging of constituents nor the threat of losing the seat.

An odd game is played out by MPs contemplating retirement. Most announce their intention to resign in good time for their constituency party to re-select. They lose the bargaining chip of securing a passage to the Lords. The Tories have the twin bribes of the Lords and Knighthoods on offer for the same purpose.

While the hereditary principle is not defensible, there will be new opportunities for ex-MPs to find a place in the Lords. The present crop are exceptionally vigorous and powerful advocates for causes they fought over in the Commons.

How to Resign

Leaving for career reasons or financial improvement is forgiven only under very exceptional circumstances. By-elections are painful and expensive for party and constituents. They consume party energies and empty the coffers.

Now there are few health reason for going. If Stephen Hawking can be a brilliant astro-physicist with very little of him functioning except his brain, MPs can struggle on. Infirmities of the body and fading mental powers are compensated by reasonably financed staff and equipment.

Staff can do a great deal to keep the work free-wheeling along until the election. Fax machines and computer modems allow a bedridden MP to complete much of the work. The House does compensate for disability. David Blunkett has an office allowance at three times the going rate to pay for his specialist braille translators and extra staff. Although the process is lengthy, requiring a vote in the House, funds would be found to assist a seriously ill MP to continue working.

When there is no other choice, application has to be made for a job either for the Manor of Northstead or the Chiltern Hundreds. Retiring MPs apply in turn for each one. With Neil Kinnock it was the Manor of Northstead. The next one will be the Chiltern Hundreds.

Perhaps the best named place for extinct politicians to retire in is the village of Dunraven.

Glossary of Terms

Adjournment Debate. At the end of each day and on Wednesday mornings opportunities are provided for a Member to speak for approximately 30 minutes to 90 minutes on an issue of their choice and receive a reply from the appropriate Minister. Because many Members want to utilise this device, the issues are selected by ballot. The Speaker has discretion to choose one Member and one subject from those submitted.

All-Party Groups. In each party there are Committees which meet regularly to discuss various policy areas. For some subjects, Members form groups across party boundaries. These are mostly on subjects which do not excite great inter-party hostility.

Bill. The name given to an Act before it is passed in Parliament.

Clerks. Staff of the House, equivalent to senior civil servants. They advise the Chair, Committees and individual Members on procedure and draft Select Committee reports.

Deputies to The Speaker of The House. Three deputies assist the Speaker. They are balanced in terms of party and subject to the same limitations on voting.

Early Day Motions (EDMs). Any Member can table a motion at any time. Members use the tabling of motions to advertise an issue or demonstrate the extent of support for an idea by the number of Members who sign it. The name derives from the fact that such motions are tabled for debate on an 'early day'. They are very rarely debated. Insiders refer to the Early Day Motions as graffiti.

Frontbencher. Members who speak not only for themselves, but for the Government and the Opposition parties. Such Members speak from the front benches while other Members speak from behind or below the gangway.

Green Papers. Government publications stating policy in provisional form for consultation.

Guillotine. Officially known as a 'timetable motion'. The Government institutes this when they want to limit the time allowed for a debate.

Hansard. The daily published verbatim report of speeches in Parliament plus answers to Written Questions.

House of Lords. the Second Chamber is made up of hereditary members and others based on party patronage. After a Bill has passed through the House of Commons, the Lords undertake a similar process of scrutiny to that which occurred in the House of Commons. A Bill will not receive the Royal Assent and become an Act until both Houses pass the same text of the Bill. Lords hold no authority in the passing of legislation on finance.

Leader of the House. Also has the grand title of Lord President of the Council. His task is to oversee the progress of Government business, liaise with opposition parties and act as the conscience of the House. Qualifications for the job are experience in Government at a senior level, wide respect from all quarters of the House and an amiable sense of humour. Part of the job is to chair the increasingly vital Committee on Standards and Privilege. The two best leaders in recent years have been John Biffen and Tony Newton.

Ministers. There are three main grades of Ministers. i) Ministers in charge of a Department of State. These Ministers are almost always members of the Cabinet. ii) Ministers of State, holding responsibilities for part of a Department under the Secretary of State. iii) Parliamentary Secretaries, also holding responsibilities for part of a Department under the Secretary of State, but lower on the ladder and paid less.

Order Paper. The daily programme for the Commons which lists in order the debates and Oral Questions of the day, Written Questions due for answer and submitted the previous day; new EDMs and recent signatories to existing EDMs are listed.

Pairing. Members in opposing parties commonly 'pair' with each other, both agreeing not to vote on a specific day so that one or both Members can be absent without affecting the outcome of the division. Most Members try to have a regular 'pair' with whom they make arrangements each week.

Parliamentary Private Secretary (PPS). They are not Ministers and are not paid. Their role varies according to the wishes of the Minister they serve.

P.O.S.T.: Parliamentary Office of Science and Technology provides members with an overview of issues arising from science and technology.

Prime Minister's Question Time. Questions are submitted in advance and ostensibly ask what the Prime Minister's engagements are for the day. This allows supplementary questions on issues that are pertinent to the day. Special privileges are accorded to the Leader of the Opposition to ask three questions. This ensuing dogfight between the Government and the Opposition is a Parliamentary experience much loved by the media and mocked by the public.

Private Legislation. A Bill promoted by local authorities, public corporations, and even private companies and individuals. Such bills are subject to a special procedure to put their case through legal counsel to a Committee of the House.

Private Member's Bill. A Bill proposed by a Member who is not a Minister.

Private Notice Question (PNQ). Urgent matter that cannot have been foreseen can be raised with the Speaker's permission at 3.30 p.m. The form is for a simple question to be asked orally, a ministerial reply and a series of questions to the Minister from MPs on both sides of the House.

Question Time. Between 2.30 and 3.30 p.m. from Monday to Thursday Ministers respond to Oral Questions on the work of their departments. The time allotted varies from an hour for Foreign Affairs to five minutes for the Church Commissioners. On Tuesday and Thursday for a quarter of an hour the Prime Minister is on the rack. Question Time is theatre. The atmosphere is civilised when only a few Members are present, frenzied when the chamber is full.

Select Committee. Their task is normally to produce reports from the information and guidance of the House. Members sit in a horseshoe formation. The main activity is questioning witnesses who may be Ministers, civil servants, and representatives of interested organisations or simply knowledgeable individuals. Most Select Committees are department-related. The Committee chooses the area it wants to investigate. Select Committees are often free of party confrontation. Chairmanship of a Select Committee is an influential backbench role.

Shadow Cabinet. The Opposition party elects a 'parliamentary committee' allocating departmental subjects to Shadow Government Ministers.

Short Money. Cash for opposition parties to carry out their duties is named after the initiator of the system, former Leader of the House Ted Short. The amount is determined by the number of MPs in opposition parties and is paid directly to the party and not to individual Members. The 1997 rate is a £3,743 (£7.48 x number of votes x 1/200) and an additional amount for travelling expenses. In the 1992-97 parliament Labour's 271 MPs entitled it to £1,530,00 and Plaid Cymru's 4 Members brought in £22,040 for their party.

The Speaker of The House. (Currently Betty Boothroyd.) The Speaker is elected by the House and acts impartially between all parties and members. The Speaker does not vote unless there is a tie, and in that event exercises that vote according to convention, in favour of the Government.

Standing Committee. The purpose of a Standing Committee is to undertake the line-by-line scrutiny of a Bill. Comprised of fifteen to forty-five appointed members, selected to reflect the party balance in the House. A neutral chairman takes the place of the Speaker of the House. Members stand to move their amendments and make speeches for or against. Standing Committees can take anything from one sitting to several months to get through a Bill depending on its length and controversiality.

Standing Order 20. Occasionally the Speaker will allow a matter that is urgent, specific and important to be raised by a Member in a three minute speech at 3.30 p.m. under Standing Order 20. Convincing reasons must be lodged with the Speaker for this and for a PNQ before mid-day. In three minutes the Member strives to persuade the Speaker to set aside arranged business to discuss the urgent issue. The Speaker rarely agrees. Pleas are rejected without reasons. Even though they are rejected PNQs and S.O. 20s are splendid opportunities for swiftly raising matters of prime constituency and national importance.

Ten Minute Rule Bill. A Member can make a ten minute speech proposing legislation on a matter of his choice. It is rare for such a Bill to become a law, because precedence is given to Bills under alternative procedures. However, Members value this opportunity to air an issue at a time which gains popular media coverage.

Whip. This word has two meanings: i) a piece of paper which Members receive each week from their party telling them the business for the following week. The importance of the issue and the amount of pressure put on a Member to vote with his party is indicated by a one, two, or three line whip. ii) Whips are Members appointed to try to ensure that all the Members of their party vote according to the party's policy. The influence of the Whips depends on the weakness, or ambition, of the Member being persuaded.

White Papers. Government publications stating a firmer policy than Green Papers in a provisional form.

Written Question. If a Member does not wish to expose an issue or attack the Government, but is only interested in obtaining information, a question is submitted for written answers. These answers are printed in *Hansard*. Through skillful and persistent written questions a Member can extract useful information from the Government. However, a Minister is not obligated to answer a question. He may excuse himself on the grounds that gathering the information would be an excessive cost or it is inappropriate to give and answer for security matters.

The Stages of a Government Bill

First Reading. Formal announcement without debate of the intention to bring in a Bill.
Second Reading. At least two weeks later, the principle of the Bill is discussed in a wide ranging debate in the Commons Chamber.
Committee Stage. Line by line scrutiny of the details of the Bill by a Standing Committee composed of Members representing party strengths in the House. Amendments are made to the Bill and new clauses added.
Report Stage. The Bill returns to the Chamber to report progress in Committee. All members may speak, add further changes, and vote.
Third Reading. Usually taken directly after the Report Stage, the Third Reading is a formal or very brief overview of the Bill's function.
Lords Stages. Follows similar pattern to Commons stages. If amended the Bill returns to the Commons to agree or reject the Lord's amendments.
Royal Assent. No Bill has been refused Assent since 1707 but procedure is still followed before the Bill becomes an Act.

Index of MPs Cited

INDEX

INDEX

MPs listed above were elected at the 1992 General Election, or at subsequent by-elections in the 1992-97 Parliament